# Biography

Christopher Whitehouse is an exceptionally qualified and experienced Chartered Planning & Development Surveyor and Expert Witness in Planning, offering a professional bespoke consultation service on a global level.

At the young age of 24 years old he took a calculated risk in setting up his own planning consultancy practice, NextPhase Development Ltd, deep within the recession. As Managing Director, his drive, motivation and sheer determination has seen his company develop into a fast growing, fresh thinking and award winning professional consultancy with offices in Staffordshire and London.

Christopher provides one stop consultancy, lobbying and advocacy services for the dynamic and fast paced commercial and retail development sector and provides Expert Witness services both to the Courts and appellants at The Planning Inspectorate.

Christopher's determination has seen him recognised by the Royal Institute of Chartered Surveyors, a highly respected institution, as an exceptional ambassador for the industry; Winning Young Surveyor of the Year in the category of Planning and Development in 2014. He is also one of the youngest people in the UK to become an RICS Accredited Expert Witness.

# Contents

## Chapter 1 – Introduction

This book has been written for the benefit of you; you the developer, you the home improver, you the builder or you the project manager. It has been written as a user friendly step-by-step guide to the overcomplicated world of planning and to provide clear guidance on how to approach planning applications and deal with local authorities in order to achieve your goals; to gain planning permission and to progress onto the more exciting parts of the projects.

Planning is overly complicated in its current form. This is due to the sheer number of parties that have input into the applications, the policies, the bureaucracy and the decision making that collectively make up the sector. Over recent years the Government has attempted to streamline the application process and make it more transparent however the subsequent confusion has only led to it becoming more complicated. There are however running themes throughout the approach you should take to a planning application irrespective of the policies in place, the makeup of the councils in charge or the changes in legislation over time. I hope that the details and guidance provided in the forthcoming chapters provides a more pragmatic and straightforward guide to the process than the current government guidance found online provides.

Some proposals are more complex than others and involve more input and organisation to achieve the planning permission; whatever route you take you will find the correct approach to dealing with the hurdles that provide challenges within the chapters of this book. Whilst the guidance should never replace professional opinion, it undoubtedly identifies where such professional advice is necessary and where the work can be done by you.

The chapters of this book also provide advice to those that have already experienced the frustrations of the planning process; whether through initial *"pre-application"* forays into the world of planning, through the frustrations of a negative decision or a stressful experience that hasn't yet resulted in a decision being made. The advice provided identifies where applications can be rescued, how significant issues can be overcome or how decisions can be challenged should you not consider them to have been made fairly.

It is often the case that we approach those first in line for projects; solicitors, architects or builders, to assist us in planning matters. More often than not the correct specialist from which to gain planning advice is a *planning consultant* or a *town planner*.

I hope that my years of experience with all types of planning applications, planning situations and planning issues under my belt whilst running a successful practice and dealing with individuals on a daily basis, I am able to provide such initial guidance in an easy to follow manner.

## Chapter 2 – What is Planning Permission?

Planning permission is essentially a decision made under law to determine what, where and how you can develop. Whether that is in relation to a simple extension of a residential property, a new house in the countryside or the creation of a new town or village, the same overarching laws apply. In each instance, the ability for you to gain planning permission under law to go ahead and do the development is assessed through the consideration of your relevant proposals against planning policies.

<u>Planning Policies</u>

Planning policies are essentially the rules and guidelines that set the parameters for the suitability of development; including issues ranging from the locational suitability of the development, the type of development that is suitable, its impact upon the environment and its design.

Planning policies are set at both a local and national level. Local planning policies are drafted and adopted by local planning authorities (within local councils), which provide specific localised policies that address developments within their jurisdiction. These policies are drafted on the influence of national policies that are set by Central Government and form the basis for which all planning policies should be based.

As such there is a filter of policies down from national to local level and within those local areas further specific guidance can be provided for specific areas of interest whether that be Conservation Areas, Listed Buildings or areas of localised other importance.

Essentially every planning permission that is granted has taken some of these planning policies into consideration in the decision. Dependent on the type of development brought forward for consideration, the planning policies that are relevant maybe singular or numerous in number and in its most simplistic form planning permission will be granted where a development is in accordance with all of the relevant local and national policies associated with that type of development.

## Different Types of Permission

There are essentially two different types of planning permission; *outline permission* and *full planning permission.*

**Outline planning permission** is the securing of the principle of development without securing any of the details of the development. An example would be where you have a plot of land and you have decided to secure with the council the principle of developing a single dwelling on that parcel of land. The size of the dwelling, the look of the dwelling, how the dwelling is accessed and how it functions in the land are not all up for consideration, it is just securing the principle of development in the first instance. When outline planning consent is granted all of those other issues then have to be secured before development can commence.

Outline planning is often used where the development is such that a developer may not want to risk the overall expense of the information needed for the planning permission and instead prefers to have the security and comfort blanket of the principle of development to hand before undertaking that expense.

**Full planning permission** is the process by which all of the main decisions and details of an application have been provided in the first instance. This provides a quicker route to moving forward with the actual development itself, as the vast majority of the important considerations will be looked at within the permission proposals. As such, the vast majority of applications are made through the full application process in order to speed up the overall programme that a developer or a home improver may have to go through before they can start work.

## Decisions

Decisions after undertaking the planning application process under either route are issued, for the most part, by the planning authority in the form of a Decision Notice which often looks like a certificate. This decision notice is issued by the local authority when they are satisfied following the application process that the development proposed is suitable, accords with the relevant local and national planning policies and can progress to the next stage.

Decision notices often identify the policies to which the development accords and for the most part provide a list of planning conditions to which the developer needs to abide by. Those conditions also provide a time limit within which you have to undertake the development.

## Planning Conditions

Planning conditions are the rules under which a development has been allowed planning permission. They are often in a list form and sometimes provide the need to undertake further work before the development actually can take place. In any instance the conditions provide a time frame under which the development needs to start, identify the plans to which the development has been granted and provide the parameters under which the developer must undertake their development in order to be compliant with planning law.

As with issues in relation to planning policy and decision notices, the use of planning conditions is detailed later on in the chapters.

## Who gives Planning Permission?

The vast majority of the time planning permissions are given by planning authorities within local councils or county councils. In each instance such decisions might come through the direct decision making powers of a nominated case officer for your application (the delegated officer) or via a decision made by a planning committee, made up of local councillors following a recommendation from a case officer. In either instance, the relationship with the decision maker can be critical in the success of gaining planning permission and as such how to make sure such a relationship is efficient, productive and ultimately successful is thoroughly discussed within the chapters of this book.

## Other Permissions

Whilst full and outlined planning permissions are the predominant routes to gain planning permission other routes and other permissions do exist. Issues in relation to developments in areas of conservation, to do with Listed Buildings or agricultural sites may all carry separate planning permissions; but whilst these permissions may undertake a slightly different route, the overall guidance within the chapters on how to successfully form, apply and gain planning permissions are still pertinent for the most part.

# CHAPTER 2: KEY POINTS

## POLICY

- Planning Permission is a decision made under law to determine what, where and how you can develop.
- Planning applications are assessed against planning policies.
- Planning policies are set at national and local level and provide rules, guidance and parameters.
- They are set at national level by government within the Department for Communities and Local Government and at local level by County and District/Borough Councils.
- Every planning permission granted has taken on board policies at local and national level relevant to it.

## PERMISSIONS

- Two predominant types of planning permission are used; outline and full permission.
- **Outline permission** secures the principle of development, with the ability to deal with some matters (*reserved matters*) at a later date.
- Reserved matters consist of access, appearance, landscaping, layout and scale.
- You can reserve or deal with as many of the matters as you wish within an outline application.
- **Full planning permission** secures all of the details of development within the application.
- **Decisions** are issued by the governing authority in the form of a decision notice, provided reasons why an application has or has not been permitted.
- Decisions are often made by a council case officer under delegated powers or by a planning committee which decides following a case officer recommendation.
- **Planning conditions** are rules under which the application has been granted permission and may require further work to be undertaken. Conditions provide a time limit and confirmation of the plans that need to be followed as a minimum.
- Sometimes more than one permission is needed; applications relating to Listed Buildings or within Conservation Areas may also require a secondary consent.

## Chapter 3 – When Do You Need Planning Permission?

In the vast majority of cases, planning permission is needed when development takes place. Development may mean building a new house, building an extension, changing an existing development in some way or changing the use of an existing building. Planning permission itself is not a straightforward or exact science, there are both a number of different rules and regulations in regards to whether planning permission is needed, and also a number of grey areas as to what extent those rules can be placed upon individual projects.

The first port of call is always to understand the overall planning requirements of a proposal. Development should never be undertaken without an understanding as to whether planning permission is needed, as whilst it is not a criminal offence to undertake work without permission it can be an expensive exercise as councils can provide enforcement notices to either stop work, remove work or issue fines for undertaking work. Therefore given the relatively straightforward nature of understanding whether planning permission is needed, it would simply be mindless to start without checking.

Whilst some developments can be undertaken using permitted development rights, which I'll move onto in more detail shortly, the vast majority of any sort of development needs to be undertaken with planning permission. This planning permission may be based on a full Planning Application, or a Householder Planning Application (whereby the work relates to changes to an existing dwelling) or for other commercial development reasons.

In the boxes below are examples of when planning permission is needed for general household, residential and commercial development.

This list refers to Section 55 of the Town and Country Planning Act 1990 (as amended) and the Town and County Planning (General Permitted Development) (England) Order 2015.

Note that this list is not exhaustive and specifically relates to development commonly undertaken by self builders. Commercial development has not been considered.

Permitted development offers the opportunity to avoid the need for planning applications in certain instances (see later on in Chapter 3).

For more specific guidance visit www.planningportal.gov.uk or seek professional advice.

## When Permission is Needed

- Demolition of buildings
- Building and rebuilding
- Conversion of a building
- Sub-division of a building
- Multiple occupation of building
- Change of use of buildings
- Change of use of land
- Change of garden curtilage
- Extensions, conservatories or orangeries
- Dormer windows
- Fire escapes
- Chimneys
- Basements
- New accesses, roads or pathways
- Introduction of new hardstanding
- Introduction of walls or boundaries
- Swimming Pools
- Tennis Courts
- Summer Houses
- Garages and outbuildings
- Use of outbuildings
- Mobile or temporary accommodation

## When Permission is NOT Needed

- Interior decoration
- Minor repairs
- Improvements or changes that do not change the external look
- Painting
- Roof repairs
- Window replacements
- Use of outbuildings when ancillary to the use of the home
- Small business use using part of the home
- Small Bed and Breakfast businesses or having a lodger
- Repairs to driveways
- Some increases to driveways
- Small scale garden planting
- Window and door insertions if they do not change external appearance
- Parking of mobile accommodation
- Most sheds or greenhouses
- Most garden furniture
- Internal services improvements or repairs.

As you can see from the boxes, it is a relatively common sense judgement as to when it might be necessary to gain permission from the council to do works. If for example we discuss home improvements and therefore Householder Planning Applications, if a proposal were to undertake a two storey extension to an existing house with new roof and new window openings, then in the vast majority of cases this would need planning permission as the proposal has the ability to impact upon not only the house itself but also the surrounding area by the way that it looks. It is therefore important that a local authority identifies in detail the scale of the proposals, how the proposals are going to be undertaken and how they impact upon the surrounding area. The same can be said with other types of home improvements. Building a large two metre wall at the front of your property with large gates, for example, may go beyond what is reasonable to build without planning permission and can be demonstrated to potentially impact upon the look of the surrounding area and therefore planning permissions, in most cases, is necessary.

In the case of home improvements where proposals make changes to the internal spaces of the property without significantly impacting upon its external footprint (i.e. it will not make changes to the exterior look of the property), then in the vast majority of cases these home improvements can be done without planning permission on the basis that they are in accordance with building regulations and structural guidance. The same applies to home improvements like guttering, new window fascias and new doors. If they are like for like replacements based on home improvements then for the most part they do not need planning permission.

You will notice that I refer to the term *"vast majority"* a lot of the time and as previously mentioned this is because planning is such a grey area. In some instances, there are sensitive locations which will be identified by your local authority. Flagging up a sensitive location may be because the dwelling in question is located within a Conservation Area or is of Heritage Listed value; in these instances even small design changes or small home improvements, such as the replacement of a door or window fascia, may have a significant impact upon that Conservation Area or the Listed Building and therefore require planning consent. It is this example which demonstrates the overall grey areas that can occur when it comes to planning permission and why it is extremely important to understand the context of the development site in relation to its surrounding area.

Whilst permitted development allows for some of these activities to be undertaken, technically without planning permission, it is a good rule of thumb to also remember that most development that extends the front elevation of a property is likely to need planning permission, even if from a size perspective it qualifies for permitted development. This is essentially due to the same reasons as larger extensions; namely the fact that, for example, the development of a porch or garage that protrudes out of the existing front of a building could, in principle, have an impact upon a larger area than the site in question as it could impact upon the streetscene or the appearance of a particular area. In that instance, it would be necessary to make sure that the local authority are satisfied that the proposal is in accordance with their requirements.

In relation to new build developments, whether residential, commercial or under another Use Class, in the vast majority of cases it will be necessary to gain planning permission before that work can be undertaken. This is to make sure that the local planning authority have the opportunity to assess that the site in question, within which the building works are proposed, is suitable for development in the first instance; that the development proposed is appropriate in terms of its location and proportionate in terms of its size, in turn meeting all local planning requirements. It is also most likely that the like for like replacement of a building with a new building would need planning permission and the demolition of an existing building in order to provide a new building would also need planning permission for exactly the same reasons. The council need to make sure that what you propose to do is something that they consider to be appropriate and reasonable.

A *change of use* application is exactly as it sounds; it is the change of use of a particular function of a building (under a planning *"Use Class"*) to another. For example, this may be the conversion of a dwelling into a shop. Whilst the application may not make significant changes to the exterior or interior appearance of a building, the change of use and function of that building has the potential to impact upon a wider area than the site itself and therefore needs planning permission. There are a number of planning Use Classes which are periodically updated and found within The Town and Country Planning (Use Classes) (Amendment) (England) Order 2015. Whilst updated permitted development laws of the last few years have allowed some of these changes from one Use Class to another to occur without planning permission, it is safe to assume that the vast majority of conversions from one to another do need permission. Overleaf I provide the list of planning Use Classes together with a brief description of what those Use Classes are.

| Use Class | Use Type | Relates to |
|---|---|---|
| A1 | Shops | Shops, retail warehouses, hairdressers, undertakers, travel and ticket agencies, post offices, pet shops, sandwich bars, showrooms, domestic hire shops, dry cleaners, funeral directors and internet cafes. |
| A2 | Financial and professional services | Financial services such as banks and building societies, professional services (other than health and medical services) and including estate and employment agencies. It does not include betting offices or pay day loan shops - these are now classed as "sui generis" uses (see below). |
| A3 | Restaurants and cafés | For the sale of food and drink for consumption on the premises - restaurants, snack bars and cafes. |
| A4 | Drinking establishments | Public houses, wine bars or other drinking establishments (but not night clubs). |
| A5 | Hot food takeaways | For the sale of hot food for consumption off the premises. |
| B1 | Business | Offices (other than those that fall within A2), research and development of products and processes, light industry appropriate in a residential area. |
| B2 | General industrial | Use for industrial process other than one falling within class B1 (excluding incineration purposes, chemical treatment or landfill or hazardous waste). |
| B8 | Storage or distribution | This class includes open air storage. |
| C1 | Hotels | Hotels, boarding and guest houses where no significant element of care is provided (excludes hostels). |
| C2 | Residential institutions | Residential care homes, hospitals, nursing homes, boarding schools, residential colleges and training centres. |
| C2A | Secure Residential Institution | Use for a provision of secure residential accommodation, including use as a prison, young offenders institution, detention centre, secure training centre, custody centre, short term holding centre, secure hospital, secure local authority accommodation or use as a military barracks. |

| Use Class | Use Type | Relates to |
|---|---|---|
| C3(a) | Dwellinghouses | Covers use by a single person or a family (a couple whether married or not, a person related to one another with members of the family of one of the couple to be treated as members of the family of the other), an employer and certain domestic employees (such as an au pair, nanny, nurse, governess, servant, chauffeur, gardener, secretary and personal assistant), a carer and the person receiving the care and a foster parent and foster child. |
| C3(b) | Dwellinghouses | Up to six people living together as a single household and receiving care e.g. supported housing schemes such as those for people with learning disabilities or mental health problems. |
| C3(c) | Dwellinghouses | Allows for groups of people (up to six) living together as a single household. This allows for those groupings that do not fall within the C4 HMO definition, but which fell within the previous C3 use class, to be provided for i.e. a small religious community may fall into this section as could a homeowner who is living with a lodger. |
| C4 | Houses in multiple occupation | Small shared houses occupied by between three and six unrelated individuals, as their only or main residence, who share basic amenities such as a kitchen or bathroom. |
| D1 | Non-residential institutions | Clinics, health centres, crèches, day nurseries, day centres, schools, art galleries (other than for sale or hire), museums, libraries, halls, places of worship, church halls, law court. Non residential education and training centres. |
| D2 | Assembly and leisure | Cinemas, music and concert halls, bingo and dance halls (but not night clubs), swimming baths, skating rinks, gymnasiums or area for indoor or outdoor sports and recreations (except for motor sports, or where firearms are used). |
| Sui Generis | Certain uses do not fall within any use class and are considered 'sui generis'. Such uses include: betting offices/shops, pay day loan shops, theatres, houses in multiple occupation, hostels providing no significant element of care, scrap yards. Petrol filling stations and shops selling and/or displaying motor vehicles. Retail warehouse clubs, night clubs, launderettes, taxi businesses, amusement centres and casinos | |

## Permitted Development

The ability to use permitted development to undertake minor works within the household, the workplace and elsewhere have been given a shot in the arm over recent years with Government changes to permitted development rights. Whilst Permitted Development via Legislative Orders, the latest of which, the Town and Country Planning (General Permitted Development) (England) Order 2015, have always contributed to the planning system I have known; the household friendly regulations of recent years have essentially been provided to kick-start the building trade again after the recent difficult years of the recession.

One of the most commonly asked questions I receive when I undertake Planning Doctor consultations at events around the country is, "does the proposal I want to do qualify for permitted development?". It is often the misunderstood notion that if development does not qualify for permitted development then it is a no go because planning permission is so difficult to get. In the vast majority of cases where clients ask if permitted development rights exist and they do not or the proposal doesn't qualify, then it is often the case that a simple householder planning application would be able to get them the planning permission that they require to undertake those works.

However, there is no doubt that where permitted development rights exist and can be used to undertake development they offer great incentives for individuals to proceed with works and/or changes of use to their time efficient benefit.

## What are they?

Permitted Development Rights are the grant of planning permission allowing for certain works including building works and changes of use to be carried out without having to make a planning application in the first instance. They are subject to numerous conditions, limitations and caveats in order to control their use, control the impact of them and to protect the surrounding area.

The Permitted Development Rights are an ever changing and ever evolving quagmire of rules and regulations that require the likes of myself to keep up to speed on an almost monthly basis. The new aforementioned Permitted Development Rights Order has been provided as recently as May 2015, however it is expected that numerous changes, additions and amendments will soon follow in this ever evolving technical guidance. At present however permitted development rights for householders have remained reasonably consistent in recent years.

As identified above there are limitations to where permitted development is relevant. Areas protected or excluded from permitted development rights include those areas that I like to call the *"difficult"* areas to achieve planning permission in; those with protected status. These sites fall under a class known as Article 1(5) Land, which covers Conservation Areas, Areas of Outstanding Natural Beauty (AONB), National Parks, The Broads, and World Heritage Sites. There are also other areas of land that are protected by a similar umbrella protection that relates to land that sits outside of National Parks but considered to be of high value to the surrounding area and beyond.

Whilst it should always be checked, a starting position should always be to expect permitted development rights to be reduced or excluded entirely, should a property or parcel of land you own be located within one of these protected areas.

In other locally prescribed areas of local interest, councils can take away any automatic permitted development rights and the council does this by making what is called an *"Article 4 Direction"*. This is a legal document showing the area affected and the rights that have been taken away. The restrictions in this instance are generally imposed on a blanket coverage basis with specific wording relating to the reason why these reductions or removal of permitted development rights have been made.

Planning Permission or Permitted Development?

If a permitted development right is in place for the work that you intend to undertake, there is no need to apply to a local planning authority for permission to carry out the work. It may however be necessary to obtain prior approval from a local planning authority before undertaking the permitted development in question. However, it should also be noted that permitted development rights do not provide automatic exemption from other regulations outside of planning (for example Building Regulations).

If prior approval from the local planning authority is necessary in advance of development, then they should be contacted to obtain this prior approval through filling out a pro forma. This form is often found on local authorities' websites, in which you can input the proposal that you wish to undertake and potentially provide some illustrations as well (this will be discussed in further detail within Chapter 4).

Prior approval means that a developer has to seek approval from the local planning authority, who specify that elements of the development could be considered acceptable before work can progress. The matters for prior approval vary and can be found within Schedule 2 of the General Permitted Development Order. A list of examples are found within the box below:

Example Matters for Prior Approval

*Householder Permitted Development Rights [this does not relate to flats or maisonettes]*

---

**Single Storey Extension (not exhaustive)**

Extensions (including previous extensions) and other buildings must not exceed 50% of the total area of land around the original house (as it was first built or as it stood on 1st July 1948).

Extensions to the front of a dwelling or to the side that faces onto a highway are not permitted development and require permission.

Extension must not extend beyond the rear of the original house by more than 6m if attached or 8m if detached (outside of designated/protected sites and until 30th May 2019 – after which it will be 3m if attached or 4m if detached).

A single storey side and/or rear extension must not exceed a height of 4m.

Materials must be of similar appearance to those of the exterior of the original house.

---

**Two - Storey Rear Extension (not exhaustive)**

Extensions (including previous extensions) and other buildings must not exceed 50% of the total area of land around the original house (as it was first built or as it stood on 1st July 1948).

Maximum eaves and ridge heights of the extension do not exceed the existing house.

If within two metres of a boundary the maximum eaves height allowed under permitted development is 3m.

Two storey extensions cannot extend beyond the original rear wall by more than 3m or be within 7m of any boundary wall opposite the rear wall of the house.

Balconies and verandas are not permitted development.

Materials must be of similar appearance to those of the exterior of the original house.

## What is the Difference?

*Prior approval* applications are much less detail orientated than a planning application would be. Essentially, prior approval requires less paperwork and just requires a simple "yes" or "no" from the local authority. It is often the case that if for any reason prior approval cannot be given, the council can provide reasons why this is the case. It is often the case that the proposal exceeds what would be allowed from prior approval and therefore it just needs to move up a rung in the regulations ladder to the planning application process.

The idea is that the process offers an uncomplicated open dialogue between the developer and the local authority, whilst allowing the local authority to have some say over the proposal that is being undertaken. However, the process should not replicate the planning application system and as such the time frame within which both the submission of the relevant form and the provision of the prior approval is significantly less than through the planning application process. This in turn, in principle, reduces the clogging up of the planning application system with minor proposals that will always be permitted.

However it should be noted that some areas where prior approval is needed may have specific planning, protected status or environmental status that require some simple works to be undertaken to demonstrate that the proposal would not impact upon them. An example of this is, if a proposal is located within an area that could potentially be impacted upon by flood risk, in that instance it could be that a basic Flood Risk Assessment has to accompany the request for prior approval having being prepared and produced by licenced hydrologists. (More on this in Chapter 4).

It is often the case that with some permitted development rights, if a developer has not heard from the council within the statutory period of time with which they would expect to hear from them, then development can proceed without any response from the local authority.

However, where in the General Permitted Development Order, it confirms that a response is needed from the local authority and they do not do this within the time frame, the lack of response can be appealed. In the same instance, if an application for prior approval is refused, the applicant has a right to appeal to the Planning Inspectorate under Section 78(1)(c) of the Town and Country Planning Act 1990.

## Permitted Development from May 2013

In May 2013 a householder friendly list of different development types were added to the Permitted Development Order which have subsequently been retained in the 2015 update with the limited caveats. Some allow development to be retained permanently but require that it is completed by a specific date, whilst others allow change of use development but only for temporary periods of time.

The following time limited rights allow developments to be retained permanently providing development is completed by 30th May 2019 in line with the 2015 Order.

## Household Development

The permitted development rights size limits for household single storey rear extensions have been increased from 4 metres to 8 metres for detached houses and from 3 metres to 6 metres for all other types of houses. However, larger extensions are subject to further consultation.

## Extensions to Commercial Property

Extensions to shops and professional serviced establishments are increased to 100m$^2$ or half of the original floor space, whichever is smaller. With this, extensions are also allowed right up to the boundary of the property unless it is a boundary with a residential property where a 2 metre gap will be retained.

The size limits for new industrial buildings within the curtilage of existing industrial buildings are increased to 200m$^2$.

## Change of Use Permitted Development

It is also possible to use time limited permitted development to change the use of offices to residential properties. However this is time limited and set to expire on 30th May 2016.

With reference to the table on planning Use Classes, it is also possible under the time limited permitted development rights, to change the Use Class of a building from one of a number of Use Classes to another, often for a limited single continuous time period. A précis of permitted development Use Class changes are provided in the table below.

| From | To |
| --- | --- |
| A1 (shops) | **A2**, or up to 150m2 **A3** subject to Prior Approval, or up to 200m2 **D2** subject to Prior Approval and only if the premises was in A1 use on 5th December 2013. A **mixed use** comprising an A1 or A2 use and up to 2 flats may also be permitted subject to meeting certain conditions. **C3** if the cumulative floorspace of the building is under 150m2 and subject to Prior Approval. |
| A2 (professional and financial services) when premises have a display window at ground level, but excluding betting offices or pay day loan shops | **A1**, or up to 150m2 **A3** subject to Prior Approval, or up to 200m2 **D2** subject to Prior Approval and only if the premises was in A2 use on 5th December 2013. A **mixed use** comprising an A1 or A2 use and up to 2 flats may also be permitted subject to meeting certain conditions. **C3** if the cumulative floorspace of the building is under 150m2 and subject to Prior Approval. |
| A3 (restaurants and cafes) | **A1 or A2** |

| From | To |
| --- | --- |
| A4 (drinking establishments) | A1 or A2 or A3 except buildings that may be defined as "community assets". |
| A5 (hot food takeaways) | A1 or A2 or A3 |
| B1 (business) | Up to 500m2 B8. |
| B2 (general industrial) | B1 |
| B2 (general industrial) | Up to 500m2 B8 |
| B8 (storage and distribution) | Up to 500m2 B1 |
| C3 (dwellinghouses) | C4 (houses in multiple occupation) |
| C4 (houses in multiple occupation) | C3 (dwellinghouses) |
| Sui Generis (casinos and amusement arcades/centres) | D2, or only if existing building is under 150m2 A3 or subject to Prior Approval. C3 if the cumulative floorspace of the building is under 150m2 and subject to Prior Approval. |
| Sui Generis (betting offices and pay day loan shops) | A1 or A2. C3 if the cumulative floorspace of the building is under 150m2 and subject to Prior Approval. A mixed use comprising a betting office or a pay day loan shop, or an A1 or A2 use and up to 2 flats may also be permitted subject to meeting certain conditions. |
| Sui Generis (agricultural buildings) | A1, A2, A3, B1, B8, C1, C3, D2, all subject to meeting relevant criteria and Prior Approval. See notes below. |

If development is proposed to be undertaken under the time limited permitted development, but it is not completed in time, it may be necessary to undertake a planning application to sort out the potential time frame discrepancy issue in order to avoid any potential enforcement action.

Where time limited permitted development is proposed to be undertaken it is important that the local authority are notified when the work has been completed.

## Permitted Development Overview

There are a number of other grey areas and individual permitted development rights that make up the General Permitted Development Order. For the most part however, the vast majority of permitted development rights that are relative to the general day-to-day developer and most pertinent to you reading this book are found above.

## Certificate of Lawful Development

In the vast majority of the cases, it is often straightforward to decide whether or not a proposal qualifies as permitted development. However, as identified above grey areas mean that sometimes the decision is less clear cut. If there is any ambiguity of whether the proposal passes the tests for permitted development a security blanket can be found, for the benefit of peace of mind, in the form of applying for a Lawful Development Certificate. This is not the same as planning permission but it is proof that the proposed building work that you intend to undertake is lawful. Whilst a fee is paid to achieve a Lawful Development Certificate and the certificate is provided by the local authority, it is a sensible way of understanding whether the proposal you intend to undertake does accord with permitted development or whether a planning application is needed.

## Finding Out About Planning Permissions and Whether They Are Needed

Whilst this book provides a qualified overview on when you need planning permission and when you do not, if you consider that the proposal you intend to do doesn't quite accord with the proposals above, then you should seek advice from one of two parties. You can contact your local authority for some advice or you can contact a planning consultant who can also offer you advice.

In my experience, however bias that may be, it would always be best to ask a planning consultant as opposed to a local authority what route your particular application needs to go down, as in the vast majority of instances the answer can be given instantly and it avoids the need to wait for a response from a local authority. My recommendation is, if you are in doubt, pick up the phone to a local planning consultant and ask them the question. They should in the majority of cases be able to answer your question immediately without any need for a cost to be provided for the benefit.

Further on in the book I will discuss the different levels of details that are needed, depending on the type of application that you need to undertake or the type of permitted development that you need to undertake.

# CHAPTER 3: KEY POINTS

**PERMISSION**

- Always check if planning permission is needed before you look to start works, it can be an expensive exercise to correct an error.
- If you are not sure if you need planning permission, contact your local authority planning department or a planning consultant.
- Some development can be undertaken using permitted development rights, without the need for permission, although the rights are regimented and should not be deviated away from.
- Recent permitted development changes have encouraged the building of home extensions.
- A Householder Planning Application is the appropriate route for applications involving changes to a house that do not qualify for permitted development.
- A buildings predominant function fits within a particular Use Class, as defined by the Use Class Order. Changing to another Use Class is a change of use; which may or may not require permission.
- Use the permitted development and planning application tables within this book to determine which criteria your development meets; if in doubt seek professional advice.
- Prior approval applications simply require a "yes or no" from the council – a more straight forward process than applying for permission.
- A certificate of lawfulness application provides confirmation that the proposal you intend to undertake qualifies as appropriate development – it provides a comfort blanket if you are in doubt about your development rights.

## Chapter 4 – The Decision Making Process

<u>The Application Process</u>

Excluding permitted development, the application process is relatively similar throughout a full application process, a change of use application and through the householder application process as well. The only real difference between a full and householder application is the length of time within which it is considered; a full application will consist of around an 8 week application period, whilst a householder application is supposed to be decided within 6.

An outline application is treated in a similar way to a full application in that it will also cover an 8 week period. The only other type of application that is meant to go beyond this target 8 week period is a major application (such as multiple housing, a site over 0.5 hectares in size or a large engineering operation) and this would expect to take a period of around 13 weeks to be decided.

For the sake of understanding the general process the following example time frame will be based on a generic 8 week planning application. However to relate this to a householder planning application you must simply reduce the time between the end of the consultation period (explained below) and the decision making period by around 2 weeks.

Once an application is ready for submission it will be submitted to the local authority electronically via the Planning Portal or through the post (more on this later) before it reaches the local authority for its validation checklist. This validation checklist is undertaken to make sure that the content of the application meets the minimum requirements in order for the local authority to be able to make a decision on it. The validation process often consists of the full plans and reports, as well as specific reporting that is relevant to the application itself or necessary to meet the local authority's requirements. Such a validation checklist is often found on the local authority's website and this should be obtained and looked at before an application is submitted; however if in doubt always seek professional advice. An examination of the most appropriate submission content will be discussed later.

It often takes up to 10 days to validate an application once it has actually been submitted and a lot of the time requests are made by local authorities for further information. If that is the case, there is no need to panic; the request for further information will not impact upon the council's opinion of your application. It is done to make sure that all of the correct items of information are provided in order to make a well-rounded decision.

This validation undertaking is often done by the council's administration support team and once the application has been validated, a letter will be sent to you or to your planning consultant, identifying the fact that the application has been validated, providing the date of the validation and the target decision date. The application will also be given a reference number, which will stay with the application throughout the process and the reference number will be that found on the grant of permission or the refusal notice at the end of the process. This reference number also generally allows you to follow the application proceedings on the council's own online planning portal, where most of the documents that you have submitted and the consultation comments undertaken throughout the application process are uploaded for viewing. You may follow the process yourself over time or it may be that you rely on your planning consultant to provide you with daily, weekly or monthly updates.

Once the application has been validated, you will be assigned a case officer to deal with the application. The case officer's name will be provided on the validation letter that will be sent to you.

The application then goes into what is called the *Consultation Stage*. This is a 21 day consultation period (however this can be extended at the discretion of the local authority) to allow all stakeholders, relevant to the application, to be notified of it and to have the ability to state an opinion on it. In the first instance, a list of relevant neighbourhood properties within the localised vicinity of the application site will be made by the local authority. These properties will receive a letter confirming that the application has been submitted and confirming the ways in which they can state their opinion on it. A site notice is often posted on the front of the property or on a nearby council owned item from which the local public can view it (often a nearby lamppost to the site), in order for people outside of the very localised neighbourhood consultation zone to have their say as well.

Further to this, within the 21-day period, *statutory consultees* will also be able to have their say on the application. For the most part statutory consultees are Government bodies, or specialist officers within the local authority team, that are duty bound to provide specialist opinion on certain matters in relation to the application. For example, should the application involve some sort of surface water drainage change, it may be that the Environment Agency would like to have a say on that proposal. Should the proposal potentially have an impact on the landscape by making a change to it (often the case when a house is built on previously undeveloped land), then the landscape officer may want to have a say to comment on any landscape changes that may be undertaken. If an application potentially impacts upon trees or biodiversity, then the council's arboricultural officer or ecological officer respectively, may want to state an opinion. This gathering of statutory consultee opinion covers specialisms across the board, on the basis that the local authority employ these specialists and can also incorporate a county council highways department, archaeologists and environmental health teams, where necessary to gather opinion.

Other statutory consultees consist of the local Ward Councillor or Councillors, who depending on the potential controversy of the proposal, may want to state an opinion on behalf of the constituents of their district. The local parish council is also considered a statutory consultee. It is often the case that during parish council meetings, applications made within the local parish are discussed within the parish's committee before their opinion is submitted to the local authority.

I will discuss the approach to dealing with statutory consultee comments and statutory consultees in general, including neighbourhood objections later in the book in detail in order to best strengthen your application.

Once the consultation comments have been sent to the case officer within the 21 day period (and often after – case officers are not particularly regimented when it comes to rejecting comments that are raised after the deadline) they are usually uploaded onto the online portal, so that when you type in your reference number into your local planning authority's website you can see a copy of the comments that have been raised.

This provides the opportunity for you or your planning consultant to respond, query or reiterate points that you feel are necessary to alleviate any issues that may have been raised by the statutory consultees.

What must be remembered is that statutory consultees are not always correct and often even when the consultees that are specialised in a certain field, their opinions are often that, an opinion. Within planning there is a significant difference between fact and assumption and whilst an opinion may be raised by a specialist it does not always mean that that opinion is correct or the only opinion that could be correct. Therefore, as we shall discuss in a later chapter, if you have conviction with a certain point that a statutory consultee disagrees with you then you may decide, or your planning consultant may advise, that you should stick to your guns and reiterate your point of view.

However, if the statutory consultation period results in the need to make some changes to your application, that you feel can be done in a relatively straightforward manner and does not result in wholesale changes to the original proposal, then it is often the case that (for example, if changes need to be made to the exterior design of an extension) changes to plans can be done quickly after the consultation period and submitted to the case officer with the request that that revised drawing would supersede the original. If that is the case then that drawing will be sent out to the specific consultee that raised the issue in the first instance and hopefully result in an agreement that the issue is overcome. This would result in an acknowledgement from that particular consultee that the original issue that they had has been overcome, allowing you to rest easy, as it would seem that that particular issue has been dealt with.

I advise that you take advantage of weeks 4 to 7 of the application process, the period between which the consultation period has finished and the decision is made, to make any changes that will strengthen or overcome any particular issues of concern within your application as raised by statutory consultees. Even if this means that by the end of week 7 you have superseded a drawing 4 times in order to get to a point where the relevant parties are happy with them then that is ok. It is important that you do everything in your power to work with or overcome issues or holding objections raised by statutory consultees, as this will only strengthen the application in the eyes of the deciding case officer.

However, this is slightly different when dealing with the parish council and neighbourhood consultations. It is my experienced opinion that it is often the best case not to respond to any objections or issues raised by neighbourhood objections or comments, or Parish Council objections or comments, as the points that are often raised are outside of the realms of planning policy. Development can often be a sore and controversial subject matter to stakeholders other than the developer that is doing it and it is impossible to please everyone with the proposal. However, if development were to completely stop because someone who lived locally to it was not very happy about it then there would be no development at all. Planning policy has to be based on an objective viewpoint that can be made using the local and national planning policies to hand. It is often the case that neighbourhood objections and objections raised by parish councils do not objectively deal with issues relating to Planning Policy. For example, the most common neighbourhood complaints are:

1) The proposal is going to impact upon the views out of the back of my house;
2) The proposal is going to devalue my property;
3) I don't like the look of it;
4) We don't need it; and
5) The proposal will impact on ecology / the highways / trees / the landscape / heritage (delete as appropriate) of the area.

In relation to 1 – 4 of the above, those points are the most often raised neighbourhood and parish council consultation objections to an application; however, all of those points fall outside of specific planning policy. The old cliché *"You don't buy a view"* is never more pertinent than in relation to Planning Policy. Unless the local neighbour can specifically raise one of those points against a planning policy that is relevant to it and address that policy in a completely objective manner, then a case officer should never take these points significantly seriously in their deliberation process, as they cannot be delivered from a position that is anything but bias against the application.

In relation to common complaint number 5; it is often the case that neighbourhood objectors are convinced that they are experts in a particular field, or because they have local knowledge of an area they are able to make an assessment as to whether an application would have a particular impact on one of those environmental factors listed above. However, a case officer can only make a judgement on the impact of an application on those specific areas based upon the qualified opinion of one of the statutory consultee specialists in that particular area or one employed on your behalf.

Whilst we will discuss tactics in relation to dealing with objections in a later chapter, I think it is important at this point just to clarify the role that consultation has within an application process. I wholeheartedly agree that in the spirit of democracy members of the public should have an opportunity to comment on applications that occur within their vicinity; however, sadly, the vast majority of the time those opinions carry little weight because of the issues raised above.

Decision Making

Following week 7, and we are working on the basis that the authority in question are particularly regimented about their 8-week application period (this is not always the case), the officer is in a position to start deliberating the application following the period of time in which the consultations have been received and your right to reply to those consultations have been undertaken.

We will discuss in a later chapter how to shape and strengthen your application to the point where you should be able to feel confident in a good result. If at this point in time the application is particularly strong, a case officer will be able to look through the file, look through the consultation responses and refer to planning policy in order to recommend a decision. If the application is being decided by the case officer under delegated powers (by which it means that the case officer makes the decision and it does not get *"called into a local planning committee")*, they will weigh up the application in the face of its appropriateness with local planning policies and if there are any policies that it does not agree they will assess if any material issues have been identified that overcome that particular policy disadvantage.

In a negative situation a case officer may look at an application and see that it does not quite accord with planning policy and cannot identify any particular items of merit that overcome the lack of accordance with those policies. If that is the case, then it is likely that a case officer will recommend refusal of an application.

It is also often the case that a case officer advises you or your planning consultant that they are minded to recommend approval, subject to some minor clarifications or changes to an application. It is up to you to consider whether you consider those changes, whether they be a reduction in floor space, a change in a layout of property or confirmation in writing that there will be a certain restriction placed upon the particular development, are acceptable in your eyes in order to tip the balance in your favour. It is not uncommon for last minute negotiations to be undertaken with a case officer in this regard and there have been plenty of times where a rushed job has been undertaken to make a last minute change to a plan in order to alleviate some officers concerns, allowing them to recommend approval and allowing them to meet their dreaded 8 week target determination deadlines.

If a case officer is minded to recommend approval for an application under delegated powers, then you can expect a decision to be issued via letter or email (depending on what your preferred chosen route of communication is) on or around the determination deadline. Sometimes a case officer is early in their decision and sometimes a case officer is slightly late in their decision, however in the vast majority of the cases the decision is made around the deadline period. As discussed in an earlier chapter that decision notice, if for approval, will come with certain planning conditions and informatives that must be kept to and include a time period within which the development must commence.

If the decision is sadly a negative one, the refusal decision will come with the reasons for refusal. Depending on the general success (or lack of) of an application the refusal reasons may be singular or numerous in number, depending on the lack of accordance with local planning policies or depending on how much you have upset the statutory consultees!

If you feel that you have a case that has been misunderstood, misrepresented or unjustly been refused by a local authority, then you have the right to appeal to the Planning Inspectorate and those appeal rights are outlined on the refusal notice. Please note that the issue of appeals are discussed at length later on in the book.

Planning Extensions

Sometimes if an application is particularly complex or you have unfortunately submitted it at a point where there are important statutory consultees or the case officer themselves on holiday, ill or away from their post for a period of time for another reason, then the application may not be decided within the targeted time frame. You may be subject to a request from the local council for an extension of time to make a decision. Sometimes if a number of clarifications or revisions need to be made to an application, but it can be done without the need to withdraw the application (more below), it may be that you can negotiate an agreement for an extension of time with the case officer in order to get those revisions done. It is often the case that the revisions that are submitted are then sent for re-consultation, by which it means that all of the statutory consultees that have been consulted the first time around will be consulted again. This may mean therefore that another 21 day extension is incorporated into the application process, but this is different every time and is subject to negotiation with the case officer.

Withdrawal

It may be that the application for one reason or another, at this particular period of time, is not gathering the support that is required from the local authority or requires some significant extra work to support it that simply cannot be done within a time of extension that can be agreed with the local authority. If that is the case, then your planning consultant or the local authority might be minded to inform you that the most appropriate thing to do is withdraw the application to allow those changes to be made. Withdrawing the application has to be done formally, via letter or email to the case officer to confirm its full withdrawal. Once the application is withdrawn you may make the changes that you need to do, or underpin the strength of your application, and resubmit it at a later date when you think it is more appropriate. If you resubmit the application within 12 months of withdrawing it then you can resubmit it without incurring another planning fee.

Please note however though that if the resubmitted application is significantly different to the application that went in the first time around, then it may be that the council consider it a completely different application and therefore subject to a further planning application fee. The easiest way to check if this is the case is to refer to the description of your planning application (the material description) found at the top of your validation letter the first time around. If the proposed resubmitted application does not accord with what we call the material description, then you should expect that the application will be treated as a completely separate application for a completely separate scheme.

So it is up to the judgement of yourself and your planning consultant to make sure that the resubmitted application is in accordance with the general development proposals of the first application (if you don't want to pay another planning fee).

Planning Fees

A planning application fee is usually calculated at the submission stage and paid before an application is validated. Planning application fees differ based on the type of application proposed and in the table below I provide a list of the most common planning fees based upon the type of application that is being proposed, as of August 2015.

# Planning Fees Registered August 2015

*Schedule of Planning Fees as of August 2015 [Not exhaustive]:*

| All Outline Applications | | |
|---|---|---|
| £385 per 0.1 hectare for sites up to and including 2.5 hectares | Not more than 2.5 hectares | £385 per 0.1 hectare |
| £9,527 + £115 for each 0.1 in excess of 2.5 hectares to a maximum of £125,000 | More than 2.5 hectares | £9,527 + £115 per 0.1 hectare |

| Householder Applications | | |
|---|---|---|
| Alterations/extensions to a single dwelling, including works within boundary | Single dwelling | £172 |

| Full Applications (and First Submissions of Reserved Matters) | | |
|---|---|---|
| Alterations/extensions to two or more dwellings, including works within boundaries | Two or more dwellings (or two or more flats) | £339 |
| New dwellings (up to and including 50) | New dwellings (not more than 50) | £385 per dwelling |
| New dwellings (for more than 50) £19,049 + £115 per additional dwelling in excess of 50 up to a maximum fee of £250,000 | New dwellings (more than 50) | £19,049 + £115 per additional dwelling |

| Lawful Development Certificate | |
|---|---|
| LDC – Existing Use - in breach of a planning condition | Same as Full |
| LDC – Existing Use LDC - lawful not to comply with a particular condition | £195 |
| LDC – Proposed Use | Half the normal planning fee. |

| Prior Approval | |
|---|---|
| Agricultural and Forestry buildings & operations or demolition of buildings | £80 |
| Telecommunications Code Systems Operators | £385 |
| Proposed Change of Use to State Funded School or Registered Nursery | £80 |
| Proposed Change of Use of Agricultural Building to a flexible use within Shops, Financial and Professional services, Restaurants and Cafes, Business, Storage or Distribution, Hotels, or Assembly or Leisure | £80 |

| | |
|---|---|
| Proposed Change of Use of a building from Office (Use Class B1) Use to a use falling within Use Class C3 (Dwellinghouse) | £80 |
| Proposed Change of Use of Agricultural Building to a Dwellinghouse (Use Class C3), where there are no Associated Building Operations | £80 |
| Proposed Change of Use of Agricultural Building to a Dwellinghouse (Use Class C3), and Associated Building Operations | £172 |
| Proposed Change of Use of a building from a Retail (Use Class A1 or A2) Use or a Mixed Retail and Residential Use to a use falling within Use Class C3 (Dwellinghouse), where there are no Associated Building Operations | £80 |
| Proposed Change of Use of a building from a Retail (Use Class A1 or A2) Use or a Mixed Retail and Residential Use to a use falling within Use Class C3 (Dwellinghouse), and Associated Building Operations | £172 |
| Notification for Prior Approval for a Change Of Use from Storage or Distribution Buildings (Class B8) and any land within its curtilage to Dwellinghouses (Class C3) | £80 |
| Notification for Prior Approval for a Change of Use from Amusement Arcades/Centres and Casinos, (Sui Generis Uses) and any land within its curtilage to Dwellinghouses (Class C3) | £80 |
| Notification for Prior Approval for a Change of Use from Amusement Arcades/Centres and Casinos, (Sui Generis Uses) and any land within its curtilage to Dwellinghouses (Class C3), and Associated Building Operations | £172 |
| Notification for Prior Approval for a Change of Use from Shops (Class A1), Financial and Professional Services (Class A2), Betting Offices, Pay Day Loan Shops and Casinos (Sui Generis Uses) to Restaurants and Cafés (Class A3) | £80 |
| Notification for Prior Approval for a Change of Use from Shops (Class A1), Financial and Professional Services (Class A2), Betting Offices, Pay Day Loan Shops and Casinos (Sui Generis Uses) to Restaurants and Cafés (Class A3), and Associated Building Operations | £172 |
| Notification for Prior Approval for a Change of Use from Shops (Class A1) and Financial and Professional Services (Class A2), Betting Offices, Pay Day Loan Shops (Sui Generis Uses) to Assembly and Leisure Uses (Class D2) | £80 |

| Reserved Matters | |
|---|---|
| Application for approval of reserved matters following outline approval | Full fee due or if full fee already paid then £385 due |

| Approval/Variation/discharge of condition | |
|---|---|
| Application for removal or variation of a condition following grant of planning permission | £195 |
| Request for confirmation that one or more planning conditions have been complied with | £28 per request for Householder otherwise £97 per request |

| Change of Use of a building to use as one or more separate dwellinghouses, or other cases | | |
|---|---|---|
| Number of dwellings | Not more than 50 dwellings | £385 for each |
| Number of dwellings | More than 50 dwellings | £19,049 + £115 for each in excess of 50 up to a maximum of £250,000 |
| Other Changes of Use of a building or land | | £385 |

| Application for a Non-material Amendment Following a Grant of Planning Permission | |
|---|---|
| Applications in respect of householder developments | £28 |
| Applications in respect of other developments | £195 |

# CHAPTER 4: KEY POINTS

## APPLICATION PROCESS

- A full/outline application takes around 8 weeks to be decided, whilst a householder application takes around 6 weeks.
- Major applications take around 13 weeks for a decision.
- An application once submitted, goes through a period of validation with the council to make sure that all of the information needed is provided. This can take around 10 days.
- Validation requirements can be found on the council websites.
- Once validated, the application will generate a planning reference number and be assigned a case officer.
- A 21 day consultation stage then commences whereby statutory consultees and neighbours both have a chance to comment on proposals. A site notice is usually posted up near or on site.
- Statutory consultees work on behalf of the council to provide specific, often technical advice to the council on the suitability of the scheme.
- Ward Councillors and the Parish/Town Council are also statutory consultees.
- Once the 21 day consultation period is complete you can respond to any issues raised by statutory and public consultees, potentially in the form of amendments to your plans.
- You do not necessarily have to respond to neighbourhood objections if they do not specifically relate to planning policy.

## DECISIONS

- Decisions are often made by an officer between week 7 and 8 and often they will advise on a decision before they officially provide it.
- An approval made by a case officer will come with the reasons for the approval and planning conditions.
- A refusal will provide reasons why the application has not been supported in relation to policy.
- Planning applications carry planning fees made payable to the council.

## EXTENSIONS & WITHDRAWALS

- If an officer cannot meet their decision deadline, you have the option of arranging an extension of time formally in writing to allow the application process to continue.
- You can formally withdraw the application at any time in writing, and may look to do so if the application requires a lot of work to gain the support it needs.
- You can resubmit an amended application if the predominant details stay the same for free within 12 months of the original submission.

## Chapter 5 – Preparing an Application

Pre-application Preparation

As discussed earlier there are multiple different types of planning applications, however in the vast majority of cases it is always advised to obtain pre-application advice. That application or advice can come from a variety of parties whether it be the local council themselves, a planning consultant or a ward councillor, or an expert that might have specific regional or specified advice that would provide assistance to the preparation work.

The local authority over the past few years have pushed the emphasis on undertaking pre-application programmes with them, on applications ranging from an extension through to a 200 home urban extension. Unsurprisingly these pre-application routes often involve a pre-application fee and a pre-agreed schedule of time in which the council will reply. In some cases, it may be that there is a set fee for an initial application letter followed by another fee structure put in place for an attendance of a site visit by a planning officer.

This fee approach to pre-applications is a relatively new phenomenon in order to generate further income for local authorities, given the problems that they have had with restructuring since the financial crisis. In previous years before the downturn pre-application advice was, in most cases, simply a case of picking up the telephone or writing a letter to the local authority and they would get back to you with some relatively straight forward advice within a couple of weeks. Now it is the case that pre-application advice will come in a much more structured format and it is often the case that the advice is not worth the paper that it is written on.

Too many times to mention, I have discussed with a client their general complaints and ill feelings in relation to the fee that they have paid to the local authority for the pre-application advice and the quality of the feedback that they have received.

It is simply the case that pre-applications, no matter if there is a fee involved or not, are not the priority of a local authority. We in the private sector do feel that if a fee has been paid for the service, then the service should meet certain expected standards. However, the case officers at the council see this differently; they simply see pre-application advice as being of secondary importance in comparison to them making decisions on live planning applications.

As such, it is often the common complaint from clients of mine that the pre-application element of the work they have undertaken consists of a relatively none site specific summary of planning policies that are relevant to their particular application. They could, if they had wanted to, obtain such advice from the local authority's website without the need for paying the fee.

It is also often the case that planning authorities do push people into thinking that they must take pre-application advice from them in order for them to seriously consider a planning application. This is a myth; this is pushed by the local authority and is simply not the case. The National Planning Policy Framework tells us that whilst pre-application discussions are encouraged, developers simply cannot be forced into undertaking them. This is an important factor to remember, as it is often the case that a more site specific, detailed and useful pre-application discussion can be had with a planning consultant who will not only identify what planning policies are relevant to the site but provide feedback in what a planning application should consist of and how to overcome any problematic policies.

The most common complaint from the non-specific list of policies that are given from local authorities in pre-application discussions, is the fact that they do not offer any solutions to the problems that they may think exist. I'm afraid this is just the nature of the beast; to date I have yet to see a local authority act in such a proactive manner that they are prepared to direct a potential developer to the appropriate route in order to overcome problems that they consider exist.

Therefore if a client comes to me to ask the question of whether they should undertake pre-application advice in order to start an open dialogue with the local authority, it is often the case of which local authority does the site relate to and what type of application is it? If it is simply a very straightforward planning application to a local authority that I know are not significantly picky in terms of their processes (there are five off the top of my head that I think are overly picky, but that is for another day!), then the pre-application stage should simply be avoided. A five-minute telephone discussion or a face-to-face meeting with a planning consultant will give you all the information you need and that information will be significantly more beneficial to the preparation of an application than that for which you would have had to pay a planning application fee for from a local authority.

If however the proposed application is a relatively complex one and it is considered by your planning consultant that it is going to take some effort to overcome planning policies that work against it then it maybe that the consultant feels that as opposed to obtaining any real beneficial information from a policy perspective from the local authority, the pre-application service is worth undertaking purely to identify and gauge any significant issues that they have and simply to open a line of dialogue with them; to allow them to be familiar at a later date when your more controversial type of application gets submitted to them.

I think that is a judgement call that you should make along with an experienced professional. However if it is simply the case that the application is of the straightforward type (a householder application comes to mind), then I would advise that you save the money that you would have had to pay on your pre-application and submit the application.

You can download a copy of the relevant local plans for your local authority from the council's website. They are generally found under the Planning and Environment section and there will usually be a section on the local authority's website called Planning Policy. Local authorities are duty bound on that front page of the planning policy site to identify what planning policies are adopted (live) at that particular point of time and are duty bound to offer a downloadable link to those policies so that you can download them onto your system and take a look at them yourselves.

Again if your application is reasonably straightforward then it is often simply a case of looking at the more generic policies to make sure that your planning application accords with them. This can be done by simply reading the new planning policy document and relating your proposal to it.

If you consider that the vast majority of the planning policy document accords with your proposal where relevant, then the chances are that the proposal will be deemed to be suitable. However if you do have any issues or any confusion in regards to the planning policy, or you consider that your application doesn't accord with some of those points raised in the planning policy documents, then you should seek professional advice. How to overcome any policies that do not accord with your development and how to treat planning policies in relation to your submission is an issue discussed later on in this chapter.

## Discussion of a Pre-application with a Planning Consultant

Call me bias, but I consider that the first port of call with most planning applications is to speak to a planning consultant about it. As discussed above, it will save a hell of a lot of time in understanding exactly what you can do, how you can go about it and how to do it in most cases without the need for a planning fee and without the onerous time process of waiting for the local authority to pick up your file. Of course, the general outcome of this is that a planning consultant would prefer to take hold of the application on your behalf and this comes at a cost. In the vast majority of cases the costs of using a planning consultant should not be underestimated, as planning is a complex system for even the simplest of applications, as you have probably recognised and is probably the reason why you have purchased this book!

A planning consultant may advise that there are specific policies that need further attention, or at this pre-application stage they may consider that it is pertinent to speak to specific statutory specialists or private sector specialists in order to gain their opinion on specific issues. One of the issues that may be relevant is that of ecology. If your proposal potentially impacts upon protected species or habitat through the demolition of a structure, the building of a structure and therefore the loss of habitat or the potential impact on protected species, then it is always advised that a licensed ecologist is bought to the table at an early stage to discuss the most appropriate method of overcoming any issues in that regard.

If for example, the site with which you look to develop has the potential for flooding, it may be necessary to speak to a hydrologist at an early stage to identify exactly what you can do and how to go about it. It is really only on the advice of a planning consultant to identify where those issues lie and which advice should be obtained at an early juncture.

Therefore, my overall advice in regards to pre-application advice, is to take on board the advice of the professionals that do not charge you a fee for the privilege. Doing so may deal with any issues at an earlier stage that may otherwise crop up later in the application process.


Using Pre-Application Advice to Shape an Application

The points that you have gathered on your application from the planning consultant or from the local authority should shape the way you tackle the preparation of your planning application. If for example, it is identified at an

52

early stage that the general approach to your application is fairly standard and there are no general issues with it, then the approach to preparation of the application will be relatively straightforward. This does not mean though that you do not have to meet the basic requirements in terms of the documents you provide for a planning submission. You are always expected to submit the correct documentation at all times, even if your application is considered a no brainer.

If the pre-application advice you have received has identified that there are issues of potential environmental concern (whether they consist of ecology, flooding, landscape, archaeology, etc.), it is important that you understand the scope of the issue at an early stage and on advice therefore take on specialist considerations to strengthen the credibility of your report. It may be simply that a specialist has to provide ten minutes of advice or it may be that they take two days of surveys to undertake; either way the pre-application advice will guide the necessity for such work and for example, by not providing a desktop archaeological assessment for a site that is known to have a potential archaeological merit, you are opening yourself up to both the application not being taken seriously and it not being validated in the first instance.

An Overview of What is Needed in your Planning Report

For the sake of clarity, we will start with the most basic of planning applications and then afterwards I will provide more specific examples of where more detailed information, reports or plans are necessary.

So, from a starting perspective let us look at an application for a two-storey extension to an existing house (that does not fall within permitted development rights). The proposed application will be a householder planning application and therefore it is necessary to provide a number of documents as a minimum; a location plan, a site plan, a plan showing the elevations and floorplans of the existing and proposed scheme, and the filled in planning application form together with the necessary ownership certificates attached (more on this later).

As a bare minimum, the planning application you propose should consist of the items above. It is then up to yourself, following discussions with a consultant or local authority, on whether you wish to provide more information in order to strengthen your application. I personally would always advise that such an application also takes on board a planning policy report, no matter how brief, in order to provide the council with the policies you consider that are appropriate to the site and to give a description of how the proposal interacts with the surrounding area.

Plans

So, as mentioned, the householder planning application needs to provide a suite of plans. The first of these plans is the *location plan* or *site location plan* as it is often called. This consists of a scale plan, usually at a ratio of 1:1250 which identifies the overall site in question in relation to the surrounding area. It is often necessary to make sure that the location plan contains at least two road names so that the local authority know exactly where it is.

A *site plan* (or often known as a *site block plan*) is also needed to support any application. The block plan provides a *"zoomed in"* version of a location plan to show particular physical constraints specifically in relation to the application area. The site plan should demonstrate the application area by way of a thick red line around its perimeter and any other land that sits outside of the planning application but falls within the ownership of the applicant should also be highlighted in blue. It is often the case that householder plans have to demonstrate, where extensions or demolitions are being proposed, how the new layout of the developed site would work. It is therefore often efficient to demonstrate the general site layout within the site plan so as to provide all the necessary information but in a more straightforward manner. This plan is often preferred by the council to be drawn at 1:500 scale; examples of both a site block plan and site layout plan are provided below.

**Example Site Location Plan**

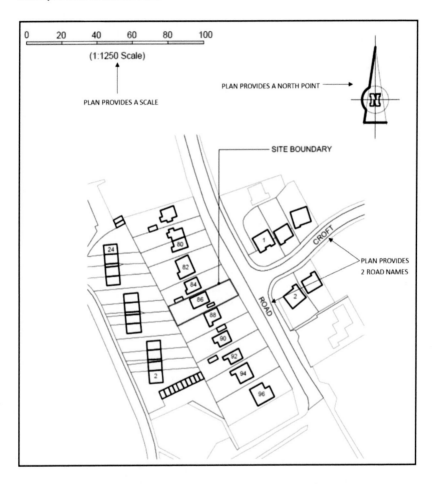

The site location plan above shows two clear street names, provides a scale bar to demonstrate the scale and provides a northern compass point. The site is identified by way of a clear red line.

The site block plan (overleaf) provides the same information but at a more detailed scale, identifying the layout proposed inside of the red line boundary and identifying other land within the ownership of the application in blue.

56

## Example Block Plan

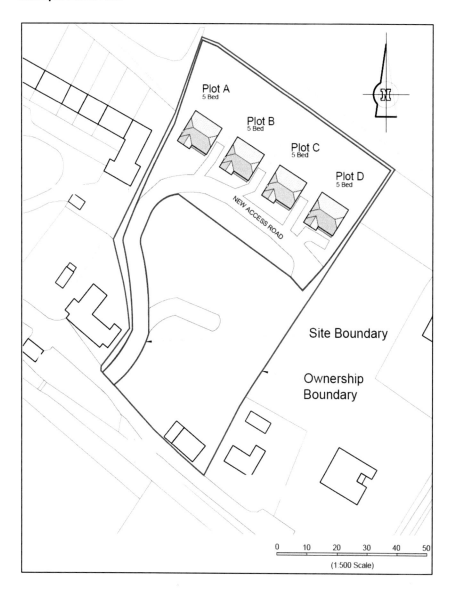

Plot A
5 Bed

Plot B
5 Bed

Plot C
5 Bed

Plot D
5 Bed

NEW ACCESS ROAD

Site Boundary

Ownership
Boundary

0   10   20   30   40   50

(1:500 Scale)

The real detail of the plans that are submitted are then provided within the *existing and proposed floor plans and elevations*. It is necessary to provide measured and accurate drawings to show the existing situation with regards to the house, both based upon all of its elevations (front, rear and sides – if semi-detached the single side is suitable) and an existing floor plan demonstrating how the rooms, corridors, doors and windows are configured throughout each relevant floor of the house should be provided. Once this has been undertaken, a separate drawing demonstrating how the proposed floor plans and elevations will work and look should also be provided. This will allow the council to compare and contrast the proposal with the existing situation and identify whether the proposal is particularly onerous or whether it is acceptable in planning terms. These plans should be provided to scale at 1:50, 1:100 or 1:200 depending on building and paper size.

Sometimes if the proposal has the potential to significantly impact upon the front of a building or on the streetscene within which the building sits, it is requested by the council that a streetscene plan is proposed which provides elevations of the existing and proposed dwelling from the front of the building, in direct comparison to the surrounding buildings within the settlement. Examples of floor plans and elevations and a streetscene plan are provided below.

## Example Floor Plan and Elevations

*Existing Elevations*

EXISTING FRONT ELEVATION
SCALE 1:50

SIDE ELEVATION (FACING NO. 84)

REAR ELEVATION

SIDE ELEVATION (FACING NO. 88)

*The elevations provide details to scale of the existing aesthetic of the property, together with exact scaled measurements of height, scale, massing, window and door positions and proximity to neighbouring dwellings.*

*Each elevation has been drafted as should always be the case unless the property is attached, when the attached side does not have to be drafted.*

*Existing Floor Plan*

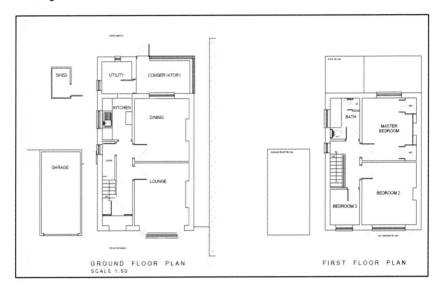

GROUND FLOOR PLAN
SCALE 1:50

FIRST FLOOR PLAN

*The existing floor plan accurately notes the existing measurements of the existing property, identifying where divisions and door spaces occur and labelling the rooms in relation to their existing function.*

*Both the ground floor and first floor floor plans have been provided and where the ground floor built footprint is single storey, the roof space of the single storey areas are shown on the first floor plan.*

*In this instance the floor plan has been drafted at a different scale to other details on the plan and therefore the specific scale is identified immediately adjacent to the floor plan.*

*Proposed Elevations*

PROPOSED FRONT ELEVATION
SCALE 1:50

SIDE ELEVATION (FACING NO. 88)

REAR ELEVATION

SIDE ELEVATION (FACING NO. 84)

The proposed elevations have shown the specific changes in terms of scale, massing and aesthetic from the existing elevations. Detailed changes to the roof scape, extensions and new windows and doors are all accurately positioned and scaled and the change in external finish to the walls is noted.

The proposed floor plan (overleaf) has undertaken the same process to the floor plans, clearly showing the changes both to the size and configuration of rooms.

The proposed streetscene (overleaf) demonstrates how the new property sits in relation to those immediately adjacent to it, to allow for contextual assessment of the impacts created by the extensions and external changes.

## Proposed Floor Plan

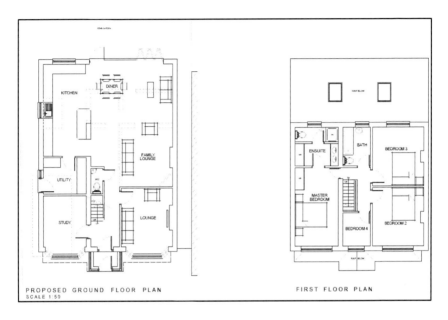

PROPOSED GROUND FLOOR PLAN
SCALE 1:50

FIRST FLOOR PLAN

## Example Streetscene

## Planning Reports

As previously mentioned we may choose to simply provide these plans and a filled in application form when submitting an application, or you may decide to provide a bit more detail in the form of a *supporting statement*. My recommendation is always to provide a statement that refers to planning policy, to demonstrate to the council that you have considered all of the potential restrictions to development and to demonstrate that those potential restrictions have influenced the design in an appropriate fashion. As such I would consider it prudent to provide a brief *planning policy assessment* which will consist of the planning policies both locally and nationally that relate directly to the development (at the minute that would be your local council's Local Plan / Core Strategy and the National Planning Policy Framework); listing those policies that are relevant in full with a sentence underneath to explain how you consider your proposal has met that policy.

With regard to design, it is likely that your council will have a design guide for housing as a separate document, again within their local planning policy section on their website. It is advised to refer to specific points in it that are pertinent, so as to demonstrate you have considered them in your proposals design.

Finally if your proposal includes the use of materials that you consider to be 'out of the norm' in relation to the surrounding area or potentially controversial, it would always be useful to take photographs of other examples of where those materials have been used successfully, preferably in the localised settlement so as not to scare off the planners when the details are submitted.

## Larger Planning Applications and the Report and Plans Necessary

We have discussed the different types of applications that can be submitted and specific detail on what should be included within specific applications is found elsewhere in the book. However as a general overview, if for example a larger scheme involved the incorporation of two new houses on land where one used to sit, then that application would be subject to further scrutiny than a relatively simple two storey extension (it would also qualify as a full planning application). As such the plans that would be required would be expected to be more detailed. However the general principles are exactly the same; a site location plan and site block plan would be necessary, a site layout plan of both existing and proposed would be necessary, and an existing and proposed situation in relation to floor plans and elevations would all be needed. More emphasis would likely be placed on the streetscene plan and it also may be necessary to provide plans in relation to landscaping and highways access. The predominant difference however comes in the form of the reporting that is necessary.

Any application that is required for a full planning permission requires a much more robust approach to the reporting that is submitted to support the application. The planning policy statement that should be written should be robust and comprehensive. Identification of all planning policies that are relevant to the application from a national and local perspective however brief the relevance, and detailed consideration of the benefits and negatives of the application have to be identified and quantified to demonstrate a balanced case in favour and in support of the application. The planning statement should identify a description of the site's location and a clear description of the proposed development identifying what is required, how it is being undertaken, what it will consists of and how it will be prepared. This statement should consider any other environmental factors that may be necessary, including the proposals impact upon landscape and visual impact, neighbourhood impact; overlooking and rights to light, highways impacts and specific impacts in relation to specialist areas.

These specialist areas may consist of issues in relation to flood risk, ecology, trees or archaeology for example, but where these issues have been identified to exist it is important that robust and comprehensive information in relation to the baseline data (what is the existing situation and why is it important) and the impact on that baseline created by the proposal is provided. Where this information is more technical it is often necessary for that information to be prepared by a specialist expert. This information should be provided in an independent report that accompanies the planning application.

In some instances, depending on the local authority's requirements, development contributions may be necessary to support an application through what is known as the Community Infrastructure Levy (CIL) or what is known as a Section 106 Agreement. A CIL contribution is a monetary contribution provided to the council upon commencement of the development, the payment of which is based upon a per square metre charge. This charge is then reinvested into the local economy, so as to in principle counteract any negative impacts that may be caused by your development.

A Section 106 Agreement is a development contribution agreed in the form of a contract that may consist of you funding a number of items (for example highway improvements) that are of benefit to the surrounding area, without a specific charge being placed against it. This contribution comes in the form of a contract and any planning permission will be subject to that contract being signed and accorded with. Section 106 Agreements are more likely to be incorporated into major schemes, whereas a CIL contribution can be incorporated into any scheme that includes the growth of residential dwellings.

As such where these contributions are required, it should be identified at an early stage by yourself and referenced in any submission. It is often the case that where CIL is particularly relevant, CIL application forms are found on the council's website and these should be filled out and submitted with the application. This will confirm to the council that you are serious about your proposal, adding an element of credibility to the proposal, but it also makes it time efficient as there is no need for the council to come back to you before validation to confirm that the forms are necessary to be completed.

Other specific reporting or approaches that should be undertaken in relation to large and other schemes are detailed later on in the book, but in principle the above provides an overview as to the level of detail that is expected in the most simplest of householder applications.


## Application Forms

Filling out a planning application form can itself be a stressful task. If you intend to submit your application electronically via the Planning Portal (which is recommended), the page by page question process does make the process more user friendly and simpler to follow if you understand the intricacies of your proposal. Most of the questions that are asked in the application form process, especially in relation to householder applications, are very straightforward and I have no doubt that you could fill them out yourself. However if you do get to the point on an application form where you are not sure what the answer is it may provide an indication that it is an element of the application that you have potentially overlooked. I would advise you go back to your documents and plans and answer the question yourself before revisiting and finishing off the application form. The element that is most often caught out by applicants who have filled out the application form themselves are issues in relation to sewerage and drainage. When preparing your plans for your application I would always advise that you understand exactly where your foul water sewage is going to and where your surface water is going to. If anything is being installed to improve the situation, understand how it will be installed and where it will be located. If you know those answers then in the vast majority of cases you can fill out the application form first time.

Towards the end of the application form you will be expected to fill out *Certificates A & B*. Certificate A identifies the fact that you are the sole owner of the land in question that you are applying for and Certificate B relates to whether there are any agricultural tenancies in place on the land in question. In either instance, if you are not the sole owner or do have an agricultural tenant on the site, it is important that you identify on the form who the other parties are and confirm on the day of the application being submitted to them that you intend to undertake the application (serving notice). This must come in written form and therefore for I suggest that, if for example, you are not the sole owner of the land for which you are making the planning application, then on the day you submit the application you also write a letter to the other interested party(s) and confirm the submission of the application. You do not have to provide reasons why you are submitting the application, but you just simply have to let them know that it is being submitted.

At the very end of the application you will be expected to declare that the information you have submitted is the truth and is accurate as you understand it, and obviously common sense dictates that if information you have submitted you know not to be accurate, then you shouldn't be submitting it.

Pre-consultation

You may considerate it pertinent to speak to other parties as you are submitting the application, to confirm that it is what you intend to do (neighbours, councillors for example) and this may be a way of reducing any tensions that may occur with those parties due to your particular circumstances. I will go on into more detail of dealing with neighbours and third parties in Chapter 7, but if you consider it wise to have a word with your neighbour to confirm that you have just submitted this application and you are giving them a heads up, there isn't much harm that can be done. A lot of the time those neighbours do appreciate the early notice.

Once the application has been submitted and you have paid for your application (via cheque, telephone or BACS transfer as advised by the Planning Portal website) then you have a period of waiting to undertake while the application is being validated. Validation itself can be a stressful and complex period. I will discuss this in Chapter 6.

## CHAPTER 5: KEY POINTS

### PRE-APPLICATION

- It may be more efficient to take your pre-application advice from a planning consultant rather than the council.
- However, if early dialogue is required due to a potentially contentious application, it is worth doing the council pre-application purely to establish a relationship.
- You can download a copy of the councils adopted planning policies from their website [search "Planning Policy"] and a copy of the National Planning Policy Framework can be found by simply typing it into a search engine.
- Use the policy documents to gauge whether your scheme is appropriate.

### PLANNING REPORTING

- As a bare minimum you need a Site Location Plan, a Site Block Plan and existing and proposed Elevations and Floor Plans if you are proposing development works.
- A Streetscene Plan, showing the relationship of the property or land with the rest of the street, is a useful addition for context.
- I would always advise including a Planning Policy Assessment, however brief.
- Specific technical reporting may be necessary for certain application sites due to issues within wider proximity to the site or specific designations; the pre-application stage or a discussion with a professional can identify what is needed.
- Community Infrastructure Levy (CIL) contributions are becoming more commonplace for new applications so be aware of the charges set in your area.

### APPLICATION FORM

- Applications are best submitted electronically via the planning portal.
- Go through the application form first before filling it in, if you are unsure of any answers specific to your application, it may be you need to revisit the issue before you submit.
- If you are not the owner of the land that your application is for, you need to notify the owner in writing at the latest of the day of the submission of the application.
- Once an application has been submitted, a fee will have been calculated and this must be paid before the application can be validated.

# Chapter 6 – The Live Application

## The Validation Period

In principle once an application has been submitted to your local authority via the Planning Portal it should take around 10 working days for the application to be validated. The submission goes through a check undertaken by the planning support team, which identifies if you have submitted all of the correct information in regards to both national and localised validation guidelines and identifies if there are any specific technical or supporting information that should be expected, given the particular location of your application.

If an application is considered satisfactory in terms of its submission, then a letter or email will be sent out to you from the local authority confirming the commencement of the application, the start date, the time frame and the case officer. If for any particular reason the validation period takes longer than the 10 working days then the start date of the application is often backdated to the 10 day point, in order to make up for the delay in terms of the validation.

The vast majority of applications will take a period of 8 weeks (13 weeks in the case of *"major"* applications) and the validation letter should identify the confirmed start date, the confirmed consultation end period and the confirmed decision deadline. Whilst local councils have their own specific targets on meeting and making sure a decision is issued by those specific deadlines, it is often the case that they do run over that period of time. As such treat the decision date as an estimation as opposed to an exact end point.

The validation of the application will generate a planning reference number. This is a reference number that is pertinent to your particular application and can be used as a search tool on the council's planning website when following the progress of your application. If you do any outside consultation to neighbours, parish councils or any other party, then it is also the reference that will be uniformly used to identify the application for all parties.

Dependent on your approach to the pre-application stage, the case officer may or may not be the same person you have originally spoken to. It is often these days, given the relatively streamlined approach to the individual planning departments that your case officer will be either the officer that generally deals with applications in your particular area or one that has the lowest case load. The case officer will more than likely be required to make a delegated decision on the proposal which essentially means that they will make the decision alone after having taken advice from their statutory consultees. The alternative is for the application to be determined by the planning committee (a collection of local councillors who determine an application based upon the recommendation of a case officer – but do not always follow the recommendation). Unless an application at the starting point is identified that a committee decision is necessary, always work on the basis that the decision will be determined by the case officer until told otherwise.

Material Description

It may be that the material description of the application that you proposed on the application form is not the one that is actually being used to detail the application on the planning records. This is because the case officer may edit the title to fit more broadly within their particular structure. It may be that they have shortened the title of the application down or beefed the application title up so as to fully describe what is being proposed. This does not have any significant bearing upon the proposal that you are bringing forward, however it does make it clear to all parties what permission is being sought after. Therefore unless you see any significant change in what you are proposing there is no need to worry about any material title changes that may have taken place.

Validation Delays

It may be that the local authority write back to you after the 10 day period to state that they cannot validate the application for any number of reasons. These reasons usually consist of the fact that the application is not complete in terms of what is needed to make the submission sufficient. In a lot of applications I tend to see that are incomplete and undertaken by members of the public, it is often that the plans are not scaled correctly or that a particular plan is missing. It is essential that, for example, all elevations are drawn up irrespective of whether what you are proposing actually impacts upon those elevations. Those plans are as much about demonstrating to the council not only what exactly is being proposed but identifying what is not changing as a result of the plans.

For example, if you are doing a rear extension that doesn't make any changes to the front elevation of the property, it is important to show this through a plan form so as to appease the council in the knowledge that the application does not impact upon the streetscene.

If for example there is an environmental issue in relation to the site, such as a need to provide an ecological wildlife report that has not been undertaken to date, this would need to be undertaken at your earliest convenience in order to validate the application. To be clear an unvalidated application has not started the clock in terms of its determination. However if you make it clear to the local authority that you are making every effort to get the information that they need as soon as you can, they are usually happy to sit on the application until the information is brought forward.

However there is technically a time frame to respond, in most cases if you do not reply to the local authority within 21 days of the non-validation letter to confirm that you are at least preparing the information they need, they will often cancel the application and return your planning fee.

If you have not overcome the validation period at the first attempt, do not panic, it does not prejudice your application whatsoever. The validation requirements of local authorities can often be overly complex and often require information be provided that has no relevance to the application. Even the more experienced of us occasionally fall short in the lottery that is the validation requirements of a local authority.

The Consultation Period

The consultation period is the 21 day (in principle) period that is the most essential when understanding if you are going to get planning permission or not. The period is essentially the first 3 weeks of any application and accounts for the distribution of the details of the application to both neighbourhood stakeholders and statutory consultees, in order to obtain their comments in relation to the application, if they have any.

At this point it is likely that a site notice will be placed upon or adjacent to your property to inform the public of what is going on. It is likely that the letters will be sent to a specific proportion of people in the local vicinity of your application site in order to provide them with the opportunity to comment on the application. There are a number of different ways that local people can comment on a planning application; it may be that they lodge their opinions on the council's online register (the same register from which you can follow the application) or it may be that they register their opinions via letter directly to the local authority. In most cases these letters are then scanned in and uploaded to the online register so that you can follow all comments that are raised.

Neighbourhood consultation will also come in the form of notifying your local ward councillor and your local parish or town council on the proposals to hand, so that they can discuss it within their appropriate forums and so that they can make a representation on behalf of the council or as councillor.


## Statutory Consultees

The statutory consultees are the specific department of expertise, both within the local authority and the wider public sector that will concentrate on particular points of your application that is relevant to their general expertise. Most authorities will take on board the opinion of a highways department, an in house ecological department (or a nationalised ecological body such as

Natural England), and Environmental Health in regards to any impacts of dust, noise or vibrations that would be considered overly onerous in comparison to normal.

Further to this if your application involves some element of focus on drainage or flooding issues then statutory bodies such as the Environment Agency will raise an opinion on the application. If it sits in an area that could potentially impact on conservational heritage guidelines then the council's conservation officer or archaeological officer may raise an opinion as well. Below I provide a table on the statutory consultees that may become relevant to your particular application and what their areas of concentration is (the list is not exhaustive):

| Technical Area of Interest | Statutory Consultee |
| --- | --- |
| Ecology and Biodiversity | Natural England |
| | Councils Ecologist |
| Hydrology, Flooding and Drainage | Environment Agency |
| | Local Drainage Board |
| Landscape and Visual Impact | Councils Landscape Officer |
| Public Rights of Way | Councils PROW Officer |
| Highways and Transportation | Highways Agency |
| | County Council Highways |
| Heritage, Conservation and Archaeology | Historic England |
| | County Council Archaeologist |
| Trees and Arboriculture | Council Tree Officer |
| Policy, Economy and Tourism | Councils Policy Team |
| | Councils Economic Team |
| | Councils Tourism Board |
| Public Representation | Ward Councillor(s) |
| | Parish/Town Council |
| Minerals and Waste | County Council Planning |
| Waterways | Canal and River Trust |
| | Inland Waterways Association |

After the period of consultation, which although theoretically is supposed to be in the first 3 weeks of an application it can often drag onto the $4^{th}$ and $5^{th}$, there is a period of time within which comments, rebuttals or amendments can be lodged in direct response to the consultation comments that have been raised. If for example there is a necessity to make amendments to your plan, then as long as those amendments don't change the material description of your proposal, you can do them during this period of time and resubmit them to the local authority to supersede the original drawings.

If these submissions have been made in order to overcome objections, the amendments will be resubmitted to the particular statutory consultees that raised the objections in order to look to remove them. Unless there has been a significant change to your proposal or it means that a statutory consultee has to significantly reassess their original comments, it is likely that any amendments will not affect the timeline of the proposal and still allow for the decision period to be reached without significant time constraints. This post consultation period can also be used in order to liaise with the council on a number of issues, whether it be development contributions, points of detail or planning policy considerations. The objective is essentially to make sure that by reaching week 7 of the proposal, if there is no need to extend the decision period (see next chapter) then you can leave a full week with no loose ends and all of the information confirmed for the officer to make a decision.

## Decision Period

The decision period is essentially between week 7 or week 8 of an application; where upon the case officer will have gathered all of the information from the statutory consultees, any amendments, revisions or rebuttals that would have been made and is now able to fully assess the application including its merits and any concerns, before reaching a decision. With relatively minor applications (such as householder applications) it is often the case that due to the officer's workload they have probably not given your application significant consideration until week 7. It is only generally at week 7, in this instance, that you may have an understanding as to the way the case officer will be making a decision, however the approach to dealing with this is discussed more in the next chapter. In most cases the case officer will look to make the decision before or on the determination deadline and will often provide an officer's report to accompany any decision. This identifies how the application has been considered and the process of decision making undertaken in terms of policy and material impacts which may result in the permission being refused or granted.

Alternatively if the application has been *"called in"* to the planning committee during the application period, then the decision determination period will be used to identify the case officer's recommendations and not necessarily provide the date upon which the application will be considered by the committee.

In terms of how to most efficiently deal with this often highly intensive and highly emotive 8 week period and the definitive splitting of time within it, I provide what I consider to be the most effective approach to general application

management in the next chapter.

# CHAPTER 6: KEY POINTS

## VALIDATION

- Validation of the application should be confirmed via letter, including the application reference number and the confirmed material description of the application.
- If for any reason outside of your control the application has taken longer than 10 days from submission to be validated, the start date is often backdated to the tenth day.
- The validation notice will provide a determination deadline, together with a consultation deadline. These are the key two dates in managing the application.
- If your application is missing something that is required for validation, you usually have around 21 days to submit it. If the information is not provided in that time, the application will likely be sent back and the fee refunded. Therefore make sure you are prepared before submission.

## CONSULTATION PERIOD

- A 21 day period within which both neighbours and statutory consultees can comment on the application.
- Statutory consultees will concentrate on aspects that relate to their specific technical role. If the application doesn't relate to their role, they will not be contacted.
- Parish/Town Councils and Ward Councillors are statutory consultees without being specialists in a particular field.

## DECISION PERIOD

- A decision is usually made by the case officer during the week of their determination deadline.
- You have the opportunity of contacting the officer to understand their likely decision before they issue it.
- If the application is "called in" to the planning committee, the officer will write a recommended decision as oppose to making it.
- The committee, made up of Ward Councillors, will make the decision by majority vote.

# Chapter 7 – Application Management

In the forthcoming chapter I provide a general approach to the way an application should look to be managed in order to gain the end result that you would want, that is the grant of planning permission. It is very much a generalised approach as the details and intricacies of each application are very much based upon their own material benefits and issues. However it is important that as the applicant or the agent working on behalf of the applicant, you or your agent are proactive and on the front foot throughout the entire application 8 week period. I can guarantee that no one will be as enthusiastic about your application as you are and therefore I consider it to be up to you or your representative to use that enthusiasm to manage the application process in the most appropriate manner. Assess the people involved, the nature of the situation and take a line that will gain results, whether that it is by taking a very relaxed and friendly approach with the local authority or whether it is by firing the proverbial rocket where necessary to get things done.

The vast majority of us professionals in the private sector do have issues with a number of elements of the existing planning system and especially the way in which applications are assessed by a local authority. However it also has to be acknowledged that with continuous public sector cuts that have been undertaken since the downturn in late 2008, local authorities and therefore local planning officers are extremely stretched in terms of their caseloads and are often inexperienced in the intricacies of specific schemes. It is therefore important you accept that they will not live and breathe the application as you will. Make allowances for their lack of detailed understanding of the intricacies of your scheme (until the point that they have to make a decision about it) and most importantly accept at the earliest stage that it is up to you to demonstrate your case clearly to the authority and not for them to find it within the information that you submit.

Nevertheless I refuse to make excuses on behalf of the local authorities that are non-engaging, non-proactive and stuck in their ways in relation to determining applications, often based upon an outdated or archaic understanding of planning policy. Where that is the case it is important that you are robust and forthright in your knowledge on the benefits of your particular application and how you consider the local authority need to interpret it.

Validation Management

In a previous chapter we identified that validation should take a period of 10 working days and often requires some further information to be submitted. It should also be noted that the people who generally validate applications do not have a professional working knowledge of planning, but they essentially work from a checklist to assess whether the application you are proposing has provided enough information in relation to it. The people who validate the application are not the ones that make the decision on the application and it is therefore important that you concentrate in the very the short term on just getting the application validated. From a starting perspective if the application has not been validated after the 10 working day period, it is important that you chase up the local authority to understand where the time frame sits; whether that is by telephone or email. My advice would be to nip the issue in the bud straightaway, pick up the phone and contact the local authority to understand where the application sits in terms of the time frame. Nothing is more immediate in providing clarity on a situation than a phone call, an email is too easy to avoid!

If upon a conversation it is clear that the application in principle is fine but it is just taking time to be validated for reasons outside of your control, then it is important that you are persistent in making sure that the application is validated as soon as it is possible. If that means contacting the local authority every day until it is validated then by all means do it. As I mentioned in the previous chapter, such an approach does not prejudice the decision making process as it is a different department that deals with it.

If further information is required then you need to take a view as to whether the request for information is reasonable or unreasonable. In most cases the request for information is due to an error on the submission or a lack of technical documentation, but in other cases it does involve the request for further information that may not have been considered to be necessary when you set out to plan your submission. It may be that the planning support officer who is validating the application is being overzealous in what is required, whether that is due to following a by the book approach or whether that is due to a lack of understanding of the scheme. If you consider that to be the case then you must protest on the requirement of the extra work and request that the support officer liaise with the development control department (the planning department) to assess if that information is really necessary. In most situations if your gut feeling is that that information is an over provision then the case officer may also agree with this as well.

If you accept that you need to provide further information it is important that you do this by the earliest possible date that you can, in order to maintain the momentum that may have been built up behind your application to date. As previously noted usually there is a period of about 21 days within which this information is required. If it is clear that this information is going to take longer than 21 days to submit, it is important that you contact the planning support officer to confirm that the information is being prepared but it will take longer. At least then the application will not be returned and your planning fee refunded so that you have to start the application process all over again.

Once that extra information has been submitted it is important that you continuously contact the council to gee them up into validating the application.

Once the application has been confirmed as validated, a planning reference number generated and a case officer assigned, then the fun with application really begins.

Consultation Management

As I stated in the previous chapter the consultation period is often the most important period for the application. What is discussed, negotiated and overcome during these 21 days can essentially put the application onto the path of decision approval or refusal. One of the most common questions and worries that is put forward to me when I speak to the public, especially at my planning clinics, is that they are worried that a particular neighbour or the local parish council may object to the application and influence the decision making process. There is absolutely no doubt that the application process, when it comes to dealing with neighbours who do not want change, or parish councils can be stressful on a personal level as essentially your plans and dreams are being discussed by those people that live around you. However the most important path to follow is that which takes place within the application process. My advice to the people that I speak to is that a local authority would always give minimal weight to objections that are raised by members of the public in an application and often even those objections raised by localised authorities such as a parish council. The reason is that any objections raised in relation to planning have to be specific to planning policy that is pertinent to the application. Try not to rise to the following public complaints about your application:

**That development is going to ruin my view**

That development is going to devalue my property

The property is big enough

It would cause serious *(insert environmental impact claim)* to us all

They shouldn't be allowed to do that as they have been doing things without permission for years

It would cause serious highways issues

There is already too much development

**It will ruin the village**

These are the most common objections that are raised in any application and I see them time and time again. However they are always raised outside of specific policy to which they could possibly refer to. It is important that any objections that are raised to a planning application, if they are to be taken seriously by a local authority, refer specifically to planning policy whether locally or nationally. All of these objections above have no direct relationship to planning policy. It is therefore the case that they should not be given any significant weight in the determination of a planning application.

The other reason why a neighbourhood consultation is given very limited weight in terms of the determination of an application, is that they are generally delivered from a positon of bias. It is very difficult for a neighbour to give an objective and reasoned approach to a consultation on a development that is happening close to them as they obviously have a vested interest in the outcome of it. The most appropriate consultations are raised in an objective and formulaic manner to put specific reference to policy. It is near enough impossible for members of the public to meet these requirements.

The question that is always asked is "well why are they given their opportunity to have their say?" but that is the democracy within which we live. If it is possible for a neighbour to raise pertinent points in relation to policy then that information should be taken into consideration. When the opportunity presents itself it is often the case that the emotive comments that spring to mind are the ones that the objectors raise. Planning, whilst it may be stressful or exciting for yourself as the applicant (based upon your particular experience), the application will always be decided in a non-emotive manner. This is important, as it generally means that you have the comfort in knowing that any public protestation to your application will not be taken into considerable detail in the determination of the application.

This is not to suggest that if the opportunity presents itself that you shouldn't look to appease any neighbourhood concerns. If you have the opportunity to discuss with neighbours, ideally before they submit any responses, the merits of the application or appeasing any particular fears that they have, then this may be useful in the long term. Not so much in terms of the officer's determination of the application but in terms of making sure that if for any reason it is called in by a Councillor, that Councillor who represents its constituents, i.e. your neighbours, is not particularly influenced by any comments that have been raised.

However by far the most important consultation that will be undertaken is the advice, feedback and requests that will be made by the statutory consultees.

## Statutory Consultee Management

Earlier in the book we identified who makes up the general statutory consultee bodies that are relevant to the application. They will all be contacted during the initial 21 day period and most will respond back within 21 days (albeit some public bodies do take longer due to their caseload). If you have gone through that consultation period and all of those consultees that are relevant to your application have responded with no objections then fantastic, you have overcome the first significant hurdle in relation to the application. However in most cases at least 1 of these consultees will need either further information or changes to satisfy their issues. Again do not worry if this is the case, holding objections (i.e. objections that can be overcome with the submission of further information) are a common occurrence in planning applications and it is simply a case of digesting what has been required or been asked of you and responding to it in the most appropriate fashion. For example if clarification is required on a particular element of a scheme, a simple written response to the council via letter or email identifying who the response is directed to and what it relates to before answering the question to hand, is more than sufficient. The submission of this to your case officer will then be redistributed to the consultee in question who can then respond accordingly.

If the statutory consultee has requested further information for a particular reason, then in most cases it is important that this information is undertaken. If that requires further technical expertise, then this will probably come at a cost that you are most likely going to have to swallow. If however the consultee in question provides a holding objection in relation to an issue that your technical data has identified shouldn't be an issue, which happens a lot, you may request that the author of your technical document discusses the issue directly with the statutory consultee in order to overcome any particular objection.

For example, you may have submitted a biodiversity survey to the Local Authority which has identified that there are no protected species impacted upon by development. The council's ecologist or Natural England may have come back and suggested that the evidence entails a requirement for further investigations to be undertaken in relation to a particular protected species. However it is quite clear that your ecologist does not agree with this, therefore you should ask your ecologist to speak to the statutory consultee directly in order to provide a technical response as to why the issue is not a relevant one. In a lot of cases the discussions that are had from your consultee to the statutory consultee are very useful ones and once the situation has been explained is it often that the statutory consultee is satisfied with the response. If you have more than one holding objection that you need to overcome, then you should use all of the technical expertise that you have to hand to answer those particular questions. Most technical experts would be duty bound to discuss the points of their reports on your behalf to their counterparts as part of the terms of their instruction (however amendments and new information may require further expenditure).

It is often the case that a particular consultee can be stubborn or irrational in their approach to an application. They may require information that is considered to be excessive, irrelevant or they may just appear to be objecting to an application without any real attempt to look to overcome any issues. If that is the case then it is up to you in discussions with your representative, your technical expert or just through gut feeling to decide enough is enough in terms of submissions. If you consider that the issue is one that has already been discussed enough in detail or is irrelevant to the overall impact of your scheme, then you have the right to challenge the statutory consultee's objections. You can do this by responding directly to your case officer in relation to it and identifying that you consider that the request for the information, the approach taken by the consultee or their general lack of pro-activeness is not something that you intend to deal with anymore and you consider the issues to be dealt with. It will be up to the case officer to decide whether your approach is reasonable and whether the statutory consultee has acted in a reasonable manner.

A case officer has the final say on an application and statutory consultees are just that. They will consult and they will advise but they do not have any specific legislative say on the outcome of a planning application.

The overall aim however is to deal with these statutory consultees on an as they come basis. You may find that you are busy for the entire 21 day period in answering questions and providing further information as the issues come in. You may find alternatively that you sail through the process with no real objections raised. There is not an exact science to how complex or non-complex your application can be; I am afraid this is due to the general inconsistent nature of the planning application process. However as we have already identified no one will know your application better than you do. A statutory consultee may provide feedback based upon their very limited period of time in overlooking the submissions, but if you think that what they are requiring is overly excessive then it is up to you to draw the issue to the close and make it clear to the case officer that you will be providing no further information.

It should be noted that any submission, resubmission, further amendments and very final amendments may all take place with one single consultee throughout the life of the application, and it may be that finally the issue is only overcome when it comes to the final week of the decision. If that is the case and the case officer has raised no particular issue with it, then it should be considered that that approach is reasonable.

Overall the most pertinent advice I can give in relation to consultation application management, is to be organised and be available to answer questions at the drop of a hat. It is important that you know all of the intricacies of your case, including the technical information that you have to hand and how far that can go in overcoming any objections that are raised by a local authority. You should maintain relations with your technical experts throughout this period, so if you need to go back to them to provide more information they can do it without significant time or expense issues.

Again when it comes down to the approach to consultation, if your application has been very stressful in the consultation stage and taken a significant amount of time to overcome any particular objections this is not particularly prejudicial when it comes to the case officer's decision. If the process has been straightforward or complex through to that final week of the decision making process, the outcome is the outcome. If there are no significant objections in place at the point of that decision then the case officer will take that into consideration whether it has been hard work in getting there or not.

Case Officer Considerations

Depending on the size of your scheme your case officer may raise points earlier than the final week in relation to the specific issues of your case. For example, the case officer may request that some amendments be made in order for them to be satisfied with the scheme in policy terms. At the end of the day the case officer is your most important consultee as they are the decision makers. If they have requested amendments in order to put them in a position where they can make a positive decision, then you have to make the judgement call as to whether those amendments can be made without significant compromise for your ideal permission. If you are in any doubt as to whether the request or changes result in a scheme being permitted that does not quite meet your requirements, then seek professional advice from your representative or your technical experts in judging this.

In most cases I always say to clients that if what they are being asked to do puts them in a position where they have lost the enthusiasm for the scheme, doesn't deliver what was required or makes it unviable, then what is the point of accepting the request of the case officer. A permission which won't provide what you want it to provide in the first place is a pointless one in most cases.

Hopefully in most cases the application you have put forward, having taken professional advice along the way, is considered reasonable in policy terms anyway. Therefore the question needs to be asked as to whether the case officer's requirements are appropriate in policy terms, or whether they are simply a request for changes for reasons that sit outside of policy. If they are for reasons that sit outside of policy then my advice to clients is to always hold your ground and confirm to the case officer that that is what you intend to do.

You can confirm this in writing to your case officer and provide the reasons why you will not be making those amendments. If you confirm that the reasons you won't be making those amendments is that you don't consider the points raised to be pertinent to particular policy, then make that clear. We should remember that if a case officer refuses an application for reasons that sit outside of planning policy then you do have the right to appeal and that appeal will generally be based solely on planning policy. There is no harm in you or your representatives making it clear to the case officer, in the most professional manner, that you disagree with the approach that is being taken to the request for revisions and that you consider them to sit outside of policy.

It is often the case that once this forthright position is taken, that a case officer will back down from their position if they realise that you are aware of the *"policy is key"* approach to the decision. However sometimes human nature takes over and an irrational or stubborn decision making case officer may stick to their guns and decide that their position is the correct one. As identified above I would always advise that you stick to your guns and use the appeal system if necessary in this situation. However if you consider the amendment to be fine in delivering what you want to deliver, then by all means make that amendment.

Relationships with your case officers can often be frustrating for the reasons that we have discussed earlier; simply their involvement in the application is not as emotive as your relationship with it is. If a proactive and conducive relationship can be had with the case officer then the application will be all the better for it. However if on reflection or through professional advice, you consider that the case officer or a particular statutory consultee is being unreasonable in their approach, then stick to your guns as you have plenty of opportunity to overcome these issues both through the application process and during an appeals process.

## Decision Period Management

In most cases once you reach the period where a decision is due, you will have an understanding as to which way your application is going to fall in relation to the determination. However in some cases (and in particular in unorganised local authorities) the case officer picks up the application file on the decision date. In those situations it is not clear right up until the decision date how your application is going to go. If you are in that position, where you have not really had too much feedback at all from your local authority right up until the point of a decision date, then be braced upon the decision date day to receive a flurry of communicative exchanges with the local authority to rectify a number of issues or prepare to negotiate in relation to planning conditions that the case officer might require to support you. However if this is the situation, then with respect, you haven't really followed my advice in this chapter. If the case officer has been completely evasive up to the point of the decision date then you have not been persistent enough in terms of your request for cooperation from the local authority through the 8 week period.

In an ideal scenario these last minute flurry of exchanges or in some cases last minute plan amendments can be avoided if you have had communication with a case officer well in advance of this date. This is not necessarily easy as some case officers are hard to get in touch with or sit behind a frustrating council contact system such as the *"call back system"*, in which you request a call back which you may never get. However persistence is key and what must be remembered is that your authority provides a public service that you have paid for and therefore your entitlement to speak to the case officer is justified.

If you get to the point where the decision that is forthcoming is a refusal and there is no real negotiation to try and overcome it on that final day, then you must brace yourself and prepare yourself for an appeal if you consider that an appeal is just. If you know in advance of that particular decision date that a refusal is forthcoming, then if you catch it early enough then you can take steps to try and overcome the situation in another manner. For example, if the application is caught early enough you may contact your Ward Councillor to try and lobby him to *"call in"* the application, thereupon making the decision one that is decided by the planning committee as opposed to the case officer themselves. This gives you the opportunity to present your case to the committee and hope for a better response than that which you have received from the case officer.

If the application requires more information that is going to take a period of time beyond the 8 week period but the case officer is determined for the application to be decided within 8 weeks, you have the right to request an extension of time, which must be agreed in writing with the case officer in order to deliver the required information. This confirmed in writing approach takes the pressure off the case officer in meeting their 8 week targets whilst allowing you to provide the information necessary to properly determine the application.

If none of these options are however available and it is clear that the case officer is intending to refuse the application then you must prepare yourself for the appeal. If the refusal is based on a number of reasons, then if you have time you should look to try and clear as many of these refusals off the register as possible so as to make your appeal case as straightforward as you can. For example, if the reasons for refusal relate to an issue relating to tree protection and an issue relating to general design; then try and provide information however late as is necessary to remedy the tree protection element of the proposal. So that when the refusal is issued the only issue that has to be challenged at appeal is that which relates to the design. In that particular instance, you should be forthright before the application has been submitted to confirm that your design is suitable in planning terms anyway and therefore you can take confidence in challenging the reason at the appeal stage.

## "Called In" Applications / Applications at Committee

For one of the strategic reasons outlined above or due to the general material issues in relation to the application, the application itself may be decided by the development control committee. As we have discussed earlier, this is a selection of local Ward Councillors who talk between themselves on the merits of the application, hear from you or your representatives on what you consider to be the material benefits of the proposal and hear from any objecting parties that may have registered to speak at the committee. They will take into consideration the officer's recommendation and then they will take a vote within which the majority rules. I have a love/hate relationship with planning committees. They are extremely useful if it is clear that a case officer's mind cannot be overcome and therefore you have a fresh platform with which to state your case. However it can also work the opposite way round if an application has been called in with an officer's recommendation for approval but for reasons outside of policy the committee do not support it.

Nevertheless if your application is in with the committee it is important that you make use of your 3 or 5 minute slot with which to speak. You should refer to the merits of the application in relation to planning policy, you should refer to how you have looked to be communicative and proactive with the local authority and you should identify how you have looked to overcome any particular issues that may be apparent in relation to the scheme. If necessary you should then confirm to the local authority that you consider the case officer's approach has been incorrect in terms of policy interpretation and the reasons why this is the case. I would always advise that if you do have a professional working on your behalf then they should undertake this particular process, as they should be experienced in making amendments or revisiting any pre-prepared speech based upon *"reading the room"* or due to any issues raised by objectors who speak first.

The majority decision will result in the application being approved or refused and you can usually expect the decision notice based upon the committees decisions to be issued within 2/3 days of the committee itself.

It should be noted that the vast majority of cases applications are decided through delegated powers by the case officer. However if your application does go to committee for whatever reason you must take advantage of any potential situation that you find yourself within.

In the next chapter I look at the next stage; with either a planning permission or a planning refusal to hand.

---

## CHAPTER 7: KEY POINTS

### VALIDATION MANAGEMENT

- If validation of your application is not confirmed within 10 days, chase it up and continue to do so until you receive a response.
- If you need to provide further information, do it swiftly.
- If you are convinced that information they request for validation is inappropriate ask the support officer at the council to discuss it with the planning officer.

### CONSULTATION PERIOD MANAGEMENT

- Use your planning application reference number to follow the application online.
- Follow the consultation responses as they come in and start preparing to reply on individual issues once the consultation period is over.
- Unless neighbourhood objections carry solid planning points, ignore them, even if you are unhappy about the content of them.
- If statutory consultees raise technical points that require a response, use the consultants who provided you with original information on the issue to reply to them.
- Always respond to issues through the case officer, or at least copy them in on all correspondence.
- Maintain good communication with your case officer from the offset and try and establish a rapport if possible so that the application remains familiar throughout.
- Always maintain complete professionalism throughout all communication and try and make points in writing as much as possible. Consultees and the officer will consider the application in non-emotive circumstances so it is important for you to separate emotions from your aim of progressing the application.

## CHAPTER 7: KEY POINTS

**DECISION PERIOD MANAGEMENT**

- Be fully contactable during the decision period, and flexible enough to make last minute amendments to plans and reports as may be required.
- The last week of the application will be the most frenetic despite the work undertaken between weeks 1-7, be prepared for it.
- If a delegated decision is being made by an officer, understand where they sit with the application before they issue a decision. If they intend to refuse it, try and provide information to reduce the reasons for refusal.
- If the decision has been called in to a planning committee, identify when and where the committee is and register to speak (or ask your consultant to speak if necessary).

**COMMITTEE MEETING MANAGEMENT**

- If you are intending to represent your own case at committee make sure you register to speak.
- I would always advise using a professional if you have one, who can answer difficult questions on the spot and react to a change in dynamic during the process.
- Keep any speech focused on the merits of the scheme and how you have looked to overcome any issues that may still be alive in the correct manner.

## Chapter 8 – Post Decision and the Next Steps

The emotions experienced directly after a planning decision has been issued generally falls into one of two categories; relief and an element of excitement that a decision has been granted, or bitter disappointment that a refusal decision has been issued given the stressful period up until that decision. In either instance the work has yet to finish and both offer a path where a further focus needs to be taken before development can actually begin. In this chapter I will discuss the two routes relevant to the two particular paths in question, again providing general advice on the approach that should be taken where appropriate.

<u>Permission Granted – Discharging Conditions and Dealing with Building Regulations</u>

The grant of planning permission will come with a number of conditions and I explained earlier in the book what conditions are. It is now important to discharge them where necessary in order to allow you to commence development. Some conditions are essentially rules that do not need any further work to be undertaken but which need to be met in order to satisfy the requirements of your planning permission. Other conditions do require some work to be undertaken, those conditions are split between two; pre-commencement conditions and post start conditions. This essentially means that some information needs to be provided to the council before you can actually make a start on the development and some information needs to be provided at some defined point in the future after development has commenced.

It is important that you review your planning permission and identify where further work needs to be undertaken. Often such specification comes in the form of further technical evidence to be gathered under a particular technical avenue, such as further protected species surveys or further information in relation to the particular design of a feature. Often it is in the form of providing confirmation of the specific materials to be used for the construction (with a requirement sometimes to provide actual physical samples of the material to the local authority for inspection and approval).

Where such conditions need to be discharged, you will need to submit another application to discharge the condition, once again this can be done via the Planning Portal electronically. The most cost and time effective approach in dealing with these sorts of discharges is to undertake all of the detail that is necessary in one go, and submitting all of the information to the council under one discharge of condition application. Such an application costs, at this present time, £97 per condition submission and it is subject to a 56 day consultation period with the local authority.

Depending on the condition it is often the particular statutory consultee, depending on the technical guidance, who discharges the condition. Therefore if the condition is particularly onerous, or for example relates to ecology and a protected species survey is needed, then obviously the ecologist would undertake the work. If a specific condition relating to design was needed then you would usually instruct your architect to do such work. Once all of the preparatory information is ready to be submitted I would always suggest submitting it in one go.

Often during the 56 day period for discharging conditions a local authority will discharge the condition much earlier and this is especially the case where they are the deciding party on the details of that particular condition. It should be emphasised that the stress of the planning application in the first instance has now been overcome and the approach to conditions on the whole is relatively pragmatic and swift in comparison. In other words this element of the application should be nowhere near as stressful as the application itself.

Once the conditions have been discharged, which will be confirmed by a discharge notification letter from the council, you can start your development and if any further information or any further conditions need to be discharged during the development then they should be undertaken at the appropriate strategic time whilst the work is ongoing.

Onerous / Difficult Conditions

If you consider that a condition relating to an application is particularly onerous, you are struggling to get a discharge consent or it is clear that no amount of information would remove it and therefore it is blocking your route to development, then you have the ability to apply to vary / remove the condition in an application to your local authority. You also have the right to appeal a specific condition directly to the Planning Inspectorate. It is always advised that the first port of call is to try and come to a solution with the local authority in relation to conditions. However if it is clear that you are hitting a wall in relation to how this particular condition is being dealt with then that is what the Planning Inspectorate is there for. If a condition is considered to be overly onerous in terms of delivering development, then the Inspector would consider it suitable to be removed from the permission and as such the issue no longer remains. Alternatively the Inspector may revise or reword the condition so as to reduce the level of information you need to provide. Either way legislation is in place to make sure that conditions are not delivered either in a scattergun effect so as to be overly onerous or strategically to stop development post a permission being granted.

## Building Regulations

Whilst this book will not go into specific detail on Building Regulations as it is a different matter altogether from planning policy, it is important that any Building Regulations requirements that you need to have met are done so at the appropriate juncture and are submitted in an appropriate way to either your local public sector building control or a privatised building control body. Only once building control regulations have been accepted as being suitable is development allowed to commence. Building Regulations in itself can be a complex undertaking, however at least you are undertaking them in the security and knowledge that the principle of development is secure and it is just the design details that are in question.

<u>Planning Refusal – Planning Appeals</u>

The planning appeals system again is extremely complex and I spend a lot of my professional life working on planning appeals within Public Inquiries and Hearings. As such I will be writing another book on the intricacies of the planning appeal system and how it should be approached in the near future. However for the benefit of this book I will keep the explanation of the process, how it works and how to tackle it relatively general so as to provide a concise understanding of the system.

Planning appeals are lodged to the Planning Inspectorate; an independent government arm of planning inspectors who reassess planning applications or points of permission based upon the information submitted and the planning policy and legislation in place at that particular point in time. They are an independent and impartial body who have no direct relationship with a local authority and as such are not swayed by local politics or any other local matters that may have influenced the original decision. In order to retain impartiality throughout a case, an inspector will keep himself at a distance from both the appellant and the council. The direct point of contact is always the inspector's case officer, who gathers information on behalf of the inspector.

Planning appeals for householder applications have to be made within 6 weeks of any decision being issued, whilst permissions for full planning permission provide the right of up to 6 months to appeal. There is also the opportunity to appeal specific conditions, a specific point of a planning approval or to appeal for non-determination if an application has gone beyond the recommended decision time frame.

Any planning appeal that is submitted has to decide between the most appropriate routes; those routes consist of written representations, an Informal Hearing or a Public Inquiry. Written representations consist of an appeal that is undertaken purely in writing through the submission of information, largely electronically. An Informal Hearing takes the same approach up until the near end of the appeal time frame, upon which a 1 or 2 day informal meeting between yourself, the council, the inspector and any other third parties that are relevant, is undertaken to provide more information that might not necessarily be able to be provided in writing and to allow for the potential for compromise to be reached between all parties around a table.

The Public Inquiry route is the more intensive route and often takes the form of a 4 or 5 day inquiry, often in the form of what appears to be a court system and often barristers and expert witnesses are used to represent appellants. As such the Public Inquiry route is significantly the most intensive and costly approach to appealing an application, whereupon the Informal Hearings approach can often offer the same benefits but for a significantly lower cost. For most appeals however the written representations route is the most appropriate as it provides an efficient and cost effective approach to assessing particular issues or particular reasons for refusal that don't need verbal advocacy or discussion.

The appeal system itself is free, although obviously if you are using professional services to support your appeal there will be costs involved in relation to this. In terms of timing, an appeal can often take longer than the application and sometimes significantly longer as the time frames are often dependant on the inspector's caseload as a whole. At the time of writing the validation period of an appeal post decision is around 8 weeks before the appeal even starts. However once it is validated the approach is very regimented; a case officer will be appointed (remember they are not the inspector) and a strict time frame is put in place up to the point of decision. For the most part the inspector who will make your decision will not be appointed until the appeal is further down the line. You again submit your appeal using the Planning Portal system, with your entire application going forward including all plans, all correspondence and all supporting reports that were submitted during the entire application period being resubmitted with a list confirming what all of those items are. To supplement this, a Statement of Case should be provided which provides a concise reason for your appeal, why you consider the reasons for refusal to be unjust and why you consider the application should be supported. In terms of size, this document should really be a maximum of around 3000 words, it should be concise with the understanding that the original application will be considered in full and this is essentially just a snapshot of the reasoning for taking it to appeal.

There are significant limitations on what you can submit as new information during an appeal. If there is a particular point of rancour with regards to an environmental issue, you may be able to provide supplementary information further to what was originally submitted, however it should not be completely fresh information so as to introduce a new argument into the appeal. The appeal itself should be centred around the reasons for refusal and not stray outside of it. Your Statement of Case should provide the vast majority of the case with which you wish to put forward, however if you identify any precedent elsewhere in the form of other decisions made by a local authority or other decisions decided at appeal but relevant to your scheme, you may wish to include these as an appendices to your Statement of Case.

Once your appeal has been submitted with the Statement of Case at its front, the onus is then on the council to reply to the appeal within their regimented time frame in both the form of a standardised questionnaire to provide specific details on the application and in the form of a written response to your Statement of Case. Within this period third parties that originally either objected or supported the application through the application period have the right to provide extra information if necessary and this should be undertaken in the same period of time granted to the local authority in response to the Statement of Case.

As the appellant you then have the right to respond to any comments that have been raised by the local authority or third parties before final comments are made by both parties. This structure of time frame often takes place over the course of 8/10 weeks and at this point you should be aware of who your inspector is and if an accompanied site visit is necessary and when it will be taking place. Often an inspector will make a site visit on their own unless there are any specific issues with which they wish to discuss on site or they need permission to enter a site. At that point they will be accompanied by you or your representative and a representative of the council whereupon which a strictly enforced meeting will take place that results in a *"speak when spoken to"* approach with the inspector. No other parties may look to influence the inspector's decision, nor must any further information be submitted at this particular point in time. Once this site meeting has been undertaken a decision can be expected to be made within due course (often weeks, sometimes months). An inspector will either dismiss the appeal and therefore continue to refuse it, or uphold an appeal and therefore grant planning permission. They will submit a report which identifies the decision that has been made in the first instance, before providing a full assessment of the case and their decision making in the form of an inspector's report accompanying it. If the inspector dismisses an appeal and therefore permission is still refused, then it is up to you to review whether you want to challenge that particular appeal (in the form of what is often an extremely costly legal approach) or whether to revise the requirements of your particular permission in a fresh application. If the inspector upholds an appeal and therefore permission is granted, they will do so with conditions of planning that they will finalise (and which have often been submitted in draft by your representatives or by the council) and a planning decision issued shortly after by the local authority. At this point the route reverts back to the discharge of planning conditions.

This is very much a snapshot of the appeals system which is often a complex entity in itself, but for purposes of clarity it often provides a useful platform upon which to put forward the merits of an application to a completely impartial professional with exceptional knowledge of the planning system, without the outside influences of local politics or issues influencing the decision making process. As such the Inspectorate route is often seen as a very useful strategic tool to deliver a planning permission.

## Resubmission – "The Free Go"

For whatever reason, whether the application has been refused either at the council stage or appeal stage, or whether you want to make some amendments to an application on the basis that the material description of the permission doesn't change, then you have the right to resubmit an application within 12 months of the original decision date in order to make the changes to your permission or a permission based on those changes. So for example if the refusal of an application was for reasons outside of the material description of the application itself (due to reasons such as ecology or flood risk, etc.) you may wish to use your free go resubmission within the 12 months whilst providing new supplementary details in relation to ecology and flood risk. Therefore you are tactically looking to improve or gain a permission based on changes you can introduce without significantly changing it, and as such you get the benefit of doing so for free.

## Amendments to an Application – Material and Non-material

However you may wish to make amendments to an application that may materially change the description of the permission. This would qualify as a material amendment to your original permission and would necessitate the need for an application for a material amendment. This is pretty much the same application approach as that within which the original application would have been permitted and it is up to you to demonstrate why the amendment is necessary; if necessary providing supporting planning information to support your reasons. What you do have however is the comfort of security of retaining your original permission if the amended application is refused and you also have the security and knowledge that the principle of development has already been permitted in the past. Therefore if the material change is not overly significant to the principle of that original permission, then the chances of it being accepted should be strong.

You can also make non-material changes through a fast-tracked non-material amendment application; this is usually a 3 to 6 week process and involves an explanation of the non-material change you are looking to incorporate and sometimes a plan to show the difference between the original and the amended proposal. Non-material changes are those which can be incorporated into a scheme but do not impact upon its material description. For example, if you are looking to slightly amend the interior layout of a proposal, change the locations of its doors or make a slight change to its window position, then they may all qualify for a non-material amendment. A description of a material and non-material amendment can be found on your local authority website but if you are in doubt as to which route it falls within then seek professional advice.

I cannot emphasise enough the importance of delivering a scheme in relation to the planning permission which you have to hand. It is important that you do not open yourselves up to potential enforcement issues and as such if you are proposing to make an amendment to a scheme when it comes to the construction then don't be put off by whatever stresses you may have experienced during the original application process. A non-material amendment is a completely different experience and is often undertaken without any consultation at all.

What is clear is that after a planning permission has been granted there is still a hell of a lot of work that needs to be done before you can start the exciting job of planning the build. However for the most part, post decision work is significantly less stressful than the period of time during the application itself. The biggest frustration generally within this period is the time frame in which it takes a lot of these amendments, discharges or resubmissions to be dealt with.

## CHAPTER 8: KEY POINTS

### PERMISSION GRANTED

- The grant of permission will come with a number of planning conditions. Any conditions that require further work before commencing development should be dealt with as soon as possible.
- If there are a number of pre-commencement conditions, try and submit all of the information at once for efficiency.
- If works are needed at various points of development and even after, make sure you are aware of what is needed and when.
- Conditions are often provided by statutory consultees during the application, and they will be responsible for discharging the condition.
- Do not deviate away from what you have permission for. The permission will refer to the relevant plans and it is important that you keep to the detail shown on them.
- The council have 56 days to respond to a request for discharging conditions.
- Difficult or overly onerous conditions can be removed by way of an application to vary or remove a condition, or by appealing to the Planning Inspectorate if you are having issues getting it discharged.
- Remember that most built development also requires Building Regulations consent before you can start works. Your architect or consultant can advise.

### PLANNING REFUSAL

- A refused decision can be appealed against to the Planning Inspectorate (PINS).
- PINS are an independent and impartial governmental arm who look at refused applications based against policy and legislation adopted at that point in time.
- It is a particularly useful platform to discuss an application, if political issues have impacted upon the original decision as the arms-length approach avoids any political pressures being added to decisions.
- Planning Inspectors make appeal decisions, and they are highly knowledgeable in the field of planning.
- Appeals for householder applications have to be filed within 6 weeks of the original decision, all other applications 6 months.
- Appeals are filed via the planning portal, requiring a Statement of Case outlining the reasons for the appeal, and the resubmission of all documents submitted to the council throughout the application process.

## CHAPTER 8: KEY POINTS

**RESUBMISSIONS**

- You may instead wish to accept the original refusal and resubmit the application once you consider the reasons for refusal can be overcome. If you do this within 12 months of the decision no further planning fee is required.

**AMENDING A PERMISSION**

- You can apply to make material or non-material amendments to your application once it is permitted.
- Small design changes would qualify as a non-material amendment (NMA).
- The NMA application process is a short, usually 3-4 week process whereby if the changes are accepted as non-material, the application is usually permitted.
- A material amendment is one which varies a considerable amount of your original application. It will be subject to a full application process to consider the impacts of the changes.
- If you are proposing to make changes to your development after you have permission, it is essential that you make the changes formally via the application process, irrespective of how difficult you may have found the process first time round.
- It is always better to make sure you have 100% conviction in your plans before your original submission.

## Chapter 9 – Specific Information for Permission Types

The book has demonstrated the general approach that should be taken to planning applications from start to finish. From conception of the idea through to managing the process of supporting information, the submission and management of the application itself and what to do after the application has been decided. The planning system is complex in nature and contains a number of intricacies that are specific to the particular Use Class in question.

Earlier on in the book we identified what particular Use Classes and types of permission were in place and within this chapter I provide some general information regarding the individual elements of information you would require for your specific type of application. The list is not exhaustive but does provide a general overview as to what you should expect to be providing over and above the generalised approach I identified earlier in the book.

<u>Householder Applications</u>

The submission requirements for a householder application are very similar to those outlined in the book; you need to provide floor plans and elevations of the existing and proposed situation, together with a site location plan and site layout plan which identifies the significance of any changes being provided by your designs.

When it comes to the design considerations it is important that you take into focus the impacts upon the neighbours and the surrounding area and whether the design of the proposal would be detrimental to anyone else or the streetscape. For example, if your dwelling is situated within a row of 15 dwellings with a very formulaic and regimented design and you are proposing to incorporate a glass box, this design may be considered difficult to gain planning permission for given the existing streetscene (however not impossible!). It is therefore important in your design considerations to weigh up the pros and cons of your design and if you are proposing something which is outside of the norm or may prove contentious then make a judgement on if it is worth it from a planning and design perspective.

You also want to have in consideration the costs of developing the proposal in terms of the materials and labour costs, and the costs that can be associated with the complexity of design when it comes to Building Regulations, as generally Building Regulations cost however long it takes an architect to design the specification.

As always you will have the opportunity to make amendments throughout the application process. However the closer the application is to being suitable in the first instance, the easier it will be throughout the process. Therefore if you consider it necessary to speak to neighbours in the first instance to advise them on the proposal and gauge if they are intending to object, it may be worth it so at least to gain a fresh perspective on the potential impacts your proposal could have. However always remember that those objections to an application are given very limited weight unless they are specific to planning policy design.

The submissions process is the same as in the generalised approach, however the application will generally be decided within 6 to 8 weeks. The consultation approach is exactly the same, however it is generally rare for a householder application to be called in to a development control committee and in all likelihood the decision will be made by the case officer. Decisions will be issued in the same way, and you usually will have a period of 3 years to implement the permission that you have gained. It is likely that the application will come with some but not an exhaustive list of planning conditions. The second or third condition usually identifies the plans which are pertinent to the permission in hand and it is important that these plans are followed when the work takes place. If you need to make changes to this permission the same route in regards to amendments and non-material amendments should be followed.

If you need to appeal a decision, you have 6 weeks to file an appeal following its decision and if you wish to resubmit you have the same 12 month free go window to file that submission.

Overall the householder application route is less intensive than the full application route. However given the fact that they are usually submitted by people for their own homes, it carries an emotive element and therefore a stressful element when it comes to the public consultations. If you follow my advice throughout the book you should find that the stress in relation to the application is significantly reduced.

Full Planning Permission

Full planning permissions can cover a range of different types of applications as outlined earlier in the book, such as new build development or change of use development and overall the approach is very similar to that outlined earlier on and similar to that in the householder approach. The application period is usually between 8 and 13 weeks depending on whether it is a minor or major application and the same approach to the submission requirements and design considerations should be taken. It is often the case however that further technical information needs to be provided in full planning permissions in comparison to the householder planning application. However that extra information is discussed in Chapter 5 as to where it is appropriate. Decisions are issued in the same manner, however planning conditions can often be longer in terms of the list and more prescriptive in terms of the need to provide more information.

Appeals for full planning permission generally need to be filed within 6 months of the decision date and depending on the type of full planning permission that is required, it may be that the informal hearing or public inquiry route is preferred depending on the size of the scheme.

Some applications come with other specific requirements depending on their location and the protective status of that particular location. A parcel of land that may sit within the Green Belt or the Open Countryside itself comes with particular and individual planning policies that are especially pertinent to that site. It is often the case that development is more difficult to get permission for in protected areas such as the Green Belt or the Open Countryside and it is important that the planning argument that you bring forward is extremely robust in order to demonstrate the material benefits of your proposal. In these locations it is a balancing exercise; the balance that needs to be demonstrated is that the material benefits of the proposal outweigh the policy restrictions that work against the site. In order to define and justify that balancing act, I would always consider it necessary that professional planning consultants are used to add credibility to that particular argument. There is no doubt that protected areas are policed more thoroughly by local authorities. Generally any application undertaken in their areas provides more consultation comments and often is called in to a planning committee for a decision to be made. It is therefore extremely important that any application taken forward in this area has prepared sufficiently so as to provide all the information that is relevant and to answer any questions in advance of them being asked.

Conservation Areas

In a similar manner Conservation Areas are also applications with a different set of rules. Generally it is important in the Conservation Area that the predominant aesthetic of the area in terms of the building designs and materials are followed so as not to impact upon the Conservation Areas aesthetic. As such you may find that the architectural design stage for your Conservation Area application is more thorough and extremely important. You may also find that the designs in principle are the items that are scrutinised the most during the application and therefore the amount of revisions that are required during the period are numerous. As such it is important that homework is done on the Conservation Area in which the land falls, to make sure that the approach that is taken forward is one that can easily be supported by the local authority.

The same approach applies to Listed Building consent, however the other points that need to be made are that the Listed Building consent is issued predominantly by a conservation officer in liaison with government heritage bodies such as Historic England. In order to gain Listed Building consent it will be necessary to demonstrate that the proposal you are bringing forward will not detrimentally impact upon the reasons for the listing of the building in the first instance. Therefore if you are intending to make internal changes to a proposal that may not necessarily otherwise need planning permission, it is likely on a Listed Building that they will. Again homework needs to be undertaken as to the importance of the listing, what the listing represents and how the proposal will impact upon it. It may be necessary to discuss the proposals with the local council's conservation officer before any application is submitted and that statutory body design guidance is taken into consideration. Finally a heritage statement will be needed to identify the fact that you have considered the conservation and Listed Building principles and justified how you came to the conclusions in relation to the design that demonstrate they do not impact upon the listing itself. Listed Building consents are often less contentious with consultees as the issues generally relate to one specific consultee (the conservation officer) than a wide ranging number of them.

If the application you are proposing to do sits outside of the discussions in this chapter and relate to a differing element that can be found in the lists of application types outlined earlier in the book, then I would always advise to seek professional advice on the approach that should be taken.

## Chapter 10 – Conclusion

The planning system is a constantly evolving and ever complex myriad of red tape, local authorities, third parties and other experts who all may have a differing view and this can impact upon any application that is taken forward. As such there is no single right path that should be taken to gain planning permission. However if general principles are followed then the chances of gaining permission are stronger than otherwise.

Preparing a planning application can be a stressful and costly exercise and it is important that you have a strategic plan in mind, you know exactly what you want and you are efficient in your decision making.

Therefore I hope that the information I have provided in this book provides a user friendly guide as to the general approach towards decision making you should undertake and how to deal with specific situations during the application process as they appear. Whilst the system is complex some elements of it, such as householder applications, are relatively straightforward and will simply come down to design. The vast majority of cases in simplistic planning applications, rely upon an element of common sense. If the proposal is going to impact upon a specific person or a specific entity then for the most part that is obvious as applications are prepared. The earlier you spot the issues, the easier they are to deal with and the more straightforward your application will become.

The most important thing you can have is conviction in your application and confidence in its robustness. If you can demonstrate to yourself that your application is sufficient and should be supported, then in most cases if the guidelines as I identified them are followed, then your planning permission will be delivered.

I would always advise seeking professional help where necessary, even if it is just to provide a sounding board to make sure that your application has been prepared correctly.

I speak to hundreds of successful and unsuccessful applicants across the country every year and it is often the case that the ones who have been regimented in their approach are the ones that have gained planning permission in the first instance.

I wish you the best of luck with your projects and should you have any questions at all you can find myself or plenty of people like myself at exhibitions, conferences and lectures across the country, or via the receiving end of a telephone call or email.

# Index

121

122

# Planning Glossary

**Adopted Local Plan**  The planning policy that is live and used by a local planning authority to determine a planning application.

**Appeal**  The request for an application decision or part of a decision to be reviewed by a third party, namely the Planning Inspectorate.

**Arboriculturalist**  A professional in the practice of arboriculture, which is the cultivation, management, and study of individual trees, shrubs, vines, and other perennial woody plants.

**Article 4 Direction**  A special planning regulation adopted by a Local Planning Authority in all or part of their borough. It operates by removing permitted development rights from whatever is specified in the direction.

**Building Regulations**  Minimum standards for design, construction and alterations to virtually every building. They are developed by the Government and approved by Parliament.

**Called In Applications**  The decision of an application is taken out of the hands of the case officer to be decided by the planning committee, by way of a request by a committee member to "call in" the application.

**Case Officer**  The council employee in the planning department in charge of the management of the application and for the most part, the decision maker.

**Certificate of Lawfulness**  A certification made to confirm that the existing use of a building is lawful for planning purposes or to confirm a proposed use does not require planning permission

**Change of Use**  The change of a Use Class of a building or land to another Use Class.

**Community Infrastructure Levy**  A planning charge, introduced by the Planning Act 2008 as a tool for local authorities in England and Wales to help deliver infrastructure to support the development of their area. It came into force on 6 April 2010 through the Community Infrastructure Levy Regulations 2010.

| **Conservation Area** | An area of notable environmental or historical interest or importance which is protected by law against undesirable changes. |
|---|---|
| **Decision Notice** | The certification of a planning application being permitted or refused together with the reasons for the decision. |
| **Delegated Decision** | A planning decision made by the case officer. |
| **Design Statement** | A statement provided by the council identifying particular design expectations for an area or specific design themes within that area; or a statement provided by an applicant identifying particular design themes of an area and how they have been incorporated into proposed plans. |
| **Discharge of a condition** | The confirmation in writing by a planning authority that information submitted in relation to a planning condition is sufficient in addressing it. |
| **Dwelling** | A house, flat or other place of residence. |
| **Ecologist** | A specialist who studies the interactions of animals and plants and the environment in which they live. |
| **Emerging Policy** | The planning policy that is currently being prepared by a local authority and that is due to be adopted in the near future. |
| **Enforcement Notice** | Issued where the local planning authority is satisfied that it appears to them that there has been a breach of planning control, set by a planning permission, and it is expedient to issue a notice to remediate the issue. |
| **Expert Witness** | A person whose level of specialised knowledge or skill in a particular field qualifies them to present their opinion about the facts of a case during legal proceedings. In professional circles expert witnesses are usually recognised as such by a relevant regulatory body. |
| **Full Planning Permission** | Planning permission granted where all planning, environmental, economic and sustainability matters have been identified and reviewed at the outset. |
| **Green Belt** | A ring of countryside of varying size located around urban settlements used to restrict the sprawl of urbanised growth by restricting building within it. |

| | |
|---|---|
| **Hardstanding** | A ground surfaced with a hard material. |
| **Householder Planning Application** | A planning application made in relation to a change to an existing dwelling or its curtilage. |
| **Hydrologist** | A specialist in the field of hydrology (water and the water cycle). |
| **Informal Hearing** | Hearings are a platform in which to present a planning appeal argument to an inspector in person, without the more formal atmosphere of an inquiry. They also allow the inspector to examine important issues in depth by asking questions of the parties involved. |
| **Listed Building** | A building, object or structure that has been judged to be of national importance in terms of architectural or historic interest and included on a special register, called the List of Buildings of Special Architectural or Historic Interest. |
| **Location Plan** | A plan that shows the proposed development in relation to its surrounding properties. It must be based on an up-to-date map and at an identified standard metric scale (typically 1:1250 or 1:2500). |
| **Major Application** | Applications defined as largescale and as such requiring a longer application process; examples are applications involving 10 or more dwellings, the winning and working of minerals or development carried out on land over 0.5 hectares in size. |
| **Material Amendment** | An application to amend part of an existing planning permission that relates to an amendment to an element defined in the material description of the permission |
| **Material Description** | The full description of the planning application or permission applied for, refused or approved. |
| **National Planning Policy Framework** | National Policy published in 2012 which sets out the governments planning policies for England; consolidating and superseding over two dozen previous planning documents in the process. |
| **National Planning Policy Guidance** | Guidance issued by the government on how they expect planning policy and planning in general to be undertaken by local authorities. The guidance should be read in conjunction with the NPPF. |

| | |
|---|---|
| **Non-material amendment** | An application made to change an element of a permission that is not considered material in its importance to the local authority (by which the change would not impact on the approach taken to the original decision). |
| **Open Countryside** | Land that sits outside of defined settlements and not designated under another status (such as Green Belt of a National Park). |
| **Outline Planning Permission** | Planning permission to secure the principle of development, whist providing the option to reserve certain matters of detail to a later date. |
| **Overlooking** | Where harm is caused to the privacy of a neighbour by way of creating views that impose on that privacy. |
| **Permitted Development** | Rights to make certain types of minor changes without needing to apply for planning permission. They derive from a general planning permission granted not by the local authority but by Parliament. |
| **Planning Committee** | A collective of Ward Councillors on a committee who vote on a majority basis on planning applications following an officer recommendation. Usually the committee is used for major or contentious applications. |
| **Planning Condition** | A caveat(s) by which the application has received permission; usually a condition sets out an expiry date to implement development, the plans to which the permission has been granted and most require further work to be undertaken as a result of the permission being granted. |
| **Planning Consultant** | A qualified professional who works in the industry of planning, usually representing applicants in the private sector. |
| **Planning Fee** | The fee to be paid to the local authority once an application has been submitted, based on the standardised charging schedule available online. |
| **Planning Inspectorate** | An executive agency of the Department for Communities and Local Government who review planning decisions (or lack of a decision) once an appeal has been lodged. |

| **Planning Permission** | Formal permission from the appropriate authority to undertake works that required planning consent. |
|---|---|
| **Planning Policy** | Documents that are used by the appropriate authority to assess an application; the policies within the documents set the threshold of appropriateness of a development within a particular area. |
| **Planning Policy Assessment** | A report prepared to support a planning application which reviews the pertinent planning policy for the application and identifies if the proposal accords or is contrary to it. |
| **Planning Portal** | A government supplied online system that provides planning advice and the facility to submit an application and an appeal electronically to the appropriate authority. |
| **Post-start condition** | Conditions that require work to be undertaken at a scheduled point during development or after work has been completed, to satisfy the condition. |
| **Pre-application advice** | A formal discussion via letter or site visit undertaken with the local authority to establish their opinion on a proposal against planning policy; or a similar discussion had with a planning professional before an application is prepared. |
| **Pre-commencement condition** | A schedule of works that are required to be undertaken, submitted to the appropriate authority and approved in writing before the approved development can commence. |
| **Prior Approval** | A developer has to seek approval from the local planning authority that specified elements of the development are acceptable before work can proceed. |
| **Principle of development** | The formal acceptance by a local authority that a proposal could be appropriate, on the basis that a number of further requirements are met. An outline application looks to secure the principle of development. |
| **Public Inquiry** | An appeal to the Planning Inspectorate that discusses the appeal in a formal, court room style manner, usually with expert witnesses and cross examination, over the course of 4 or 5 days. Usually reserved for very large or contentious applications that require significant analysis. |

| | |
|---|---|
| **Reserved Matters** | Matters of detail that are not provided within an outline application, with the intention of approving them at a later date if the outline permission is granted. |
| **Rights to light** | Rights to light is a form of easement in English law that gives a long-standing owner of a building with windows a right to maintain the level of illumination. |
| **Section 106 Agreement** | Private agreements made between local authorities and developers and can be attached to a planning permission to make acceptable development which would otherwise be unacceptable in planning terms. The defined obligations are detailed within Section 106 of the Town and Country Planning Act 1990 (as amended). |
| **Settlement** | An urbanised area, whether a city, town or village, that contains a number of dwellings and for the most part is defined by a boundary set by a local authority. |
| **Site Block Plan** | A plan used to identify the proposed development in relation to the site boundaries and other existing buildings on the site, with dimensions specified including those to the boundaries. Usually provided at a scale of 1:100, 1:200 or 1:500. |
| **Statutory Consultee** | Bodies which must be consulted on certain planning applications as set out in law. When a body is consulted, they are under a duty to provide advice on the proposal in question. |
| **Streetscene** | The consideration of the way a development looks and sits in relation to its immediate surroundings. |
| **Sui Generis** | Certain Use Classes that do not fall into any particular designated use. |
| **Supplementary Planning Documents** | Research and advisory documents prepared by a Local Authority that do not make up the Local Plan under which an application is assessed, but has influenced the Local Plan policies in the first place. |
| **Supporting Statement** | A report submitted with a planning application to fully explain the development, identify development constraints and opportunities, and sets out the full argument to allow the council to consider granted permission. |

| | |
|---|---|
| **Town Planner** | A professional qualified to work within the planning industry, often found within both the public and private sectors. |
| **Use Class** | Uses of land and buildings are put into various use categories as defined by the Town and Country Planning (Use Classes) (Amendment) (England) Order 2015. |
| **Validation** | The confirmation by a Local Authority that an applications submission is sufficient enough for the authority to be able to make a planning decision on it. |
| **Variation of a condition** | An application made under Section 73 of the Town and Country Planning Act 1990 (as amended) to change or remove one or a number of the conditions attached to a planning permission. |
| **Withdrawal** | The formal removal of a planning application or appeal from further consideration by the appropriate authority. |
| **Written Representations** | A planning appeal route by which all parties (the appellant, the council and the inspector) deal with the appeal in writing alone. |